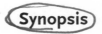

Synopsis

Anger cannot be managed or massaged — chances are you know that already. Nor can it be denied, avoided, projected or repressed with any satisfactory result. But here is the miracle: Anger can be transformed into its opposite, which is inner peace. And along with that peace come richer relationships, less conflict, a sense of well-being. If you desire peace and fulfilment, look first to anger. What you now regard as an obstacle on your life-journey will be revealed as the way itself. Not roses, sunsets or choirs, but the rough humility of anger.

It is simple, but not easy. You want peace; anger wants your attention. Give anger what it wants. Not resistance or judgment, but your unwavering attention. That changes everything.

Life gives us what we need.
It may not be what we want.
It will always be what we need.

Anger
A Message for Men

by Keith Ashford

Anger: A Message for Men

Copyright © 2009, Keith Ashford

For more information, or to order additional copies, please contact:
Keith Ashford
kashford@bell.net
menscounsellingservices.com

Published by:
Blue Poppy Press

Edited by:
Hladini Wilson

Design and Layout:
Bryan Babcock Design

ISBN: 978-0-9812970-0-2

For Marilyn,
Alexis
and Amanda

Table of Contents

Preface 1

This book owes its existence to the almost 1,000 men's groups I have been privileged to facilitate or co-facilitate since 1992.

Introduction 5

Anger was a great teacher for me. At first I didn't recognize it as a teacher. But constant companion that it was, I finally realized it had to be more than just an enemy.

Congratulations 7

The recognition of one's dysfunction is a tremendous achievement.

The Mars/Venus thing 9

The pride of the male is both self-conscious and slightly comical. We do not easily (or ever) ask for help.

Rites of initiation 13

It used to be that when boys reached puberty they were ritually separated from their mothers and families and brought deep into the wilderness to be instructed by tribal elders in the essentials of how to be a man.

The Quest 15

The quest for our missing part, for ultimate union, would appear to be the point and purpose of life.

The Fall   17

The first thing to know about this nursery rhyme is that Humpty Dumpty is not an egg, though he — unmistakably he! — is illustrated that way in the children's anthologies.

Anger is temporary   19

We reconnect with what is lasting when we recognize what is passing.

I am an angry man   21

No, you are not. You are a man in whom there is an emotion but you are not the emotion itself.

Nothing to fix   23

If everything else has failed, try this: Give up trying.

The power of observation   25

When anger arises, don't just do something — stand there.

A feral boy   27

A curtain parts, and the two of you briefly make eye contact through the glass. Suddenly the kid goes completely berserk...

Like crossing the street   29

Anger exists for no other reason than to be acknowledged. When you recognize the importance of paying attention, you will pay attention.

Control issues   31

Controlling your anger is like putting a suit and tie on a wolverine. No one is really fooled by the suit.

The real problem   34

Anger comes from nowhere other than the mind. It has no objective reality.

I have a right to be angry   36

Yes, you do, and no one is going to take that right away from you.

The four-car train to anger   37

What reads like a sequence in time is actually the content of a single moment.

Why am I angry?   39

We are never upset for the reason we think.

Only humans think   41

The reason there is no anger in the natural world is because nothing in the natural world thinks. Or needs to.

Repetitive thinking   43

Where in the jammed closet of the head is there room for love, beauty, creativity, spontaneity?

Negative thinking   45

The mind defines itself in terms of what it opposes.

Compulsive thinking   48

Forget sugar, thinking is the first addiction.

A beautiful mind   50

No such thing, really. Minds and computers have a neutral value. We can use them to write poems or build bombs.

Good news   53

You are not the mind.

Fear   55

Men whose fear is unnamed and unrecognized will often go to great lengths to demonstrate that they are not afraid.

"You" language   58

The conscious recovery of "I" language does two things: it restores clarity and power to the speaker; it gives space and freedom to the listener.

Restraint 59

As a Zen master might say, "Cut the crap."

Conscious suffering 61

Nothing burns up anger more quickly than your willingness to bear it.

Past, present, future 64

No one has ever lived in the future, and no one ever will.

My past is full of problems 66

It is technically impossible to have a problem in the past. If a problem is truly in the past, then you do not have a problem.

Q & A 68

Have you ever experienced, done, thought, or felt anything outside the Now?

The mind without a master 69

A most curious thing: The mind gives almost none of its attention to the present, to the one dimension that is real, where life actually happens. By contrast, the mind is hyperactively busy in the dimensions that are unreal: past and future, where life does not happen.

Mind your own business 72

Byron Katie says there are three kinds of business: my business, your business and God's business.

I pity the fool 74

Look, I'm not one of those guys who froths at the mouth.

Do sweat the small stuff 76

The way you do anything is the way you do everything.

A true man of no rank 78

He does not need to push, intimidate, or play the power games common to other men because he possesses his power with surety and calm self-confidence.

Personality 80

Let us be clear about what personality actually means. It derives from the Latin word persona, for mask.

One of anger's faces 82

One of the nine types is known as The Perfectionist. His anger is "dressed up" to look like a virtue.

No wax 85

It is widely believed that Roman craftsmen would wax their creations to conceal their imperfections. By this definition, a sincere man is unwaxed.

Blaming 87

Blaming is humanity's first and most enduring dysfunction.

A good man does not... 89

Argue.

Resistance 91

Either you accept your anger completely or you resist your anger completely.

The impediment of hope 94

On the strength of our hope, we endure the now. We do not embrace or transform it; we tolerate it. We wait, and we wait, and we hope.

Anger is a signal 96

Pay attention. That is all anger requires — that we pay attention to it, that we acknowledge it with our awareness.

One thing at a time 98

One of the most persistent yet least credible cultural myths is multi-tasking.

Anger needs conflict to survive 99

To sustain and validate itself, anger needs regular contact with other forms of itself.

The outer reflects the inner   101

A peaceful man embodies a state of being that anger cannot tolerate. Ironically, the angry man embodies the same state — he is just temporarily unaware of his unbelievable treasure.

The anger addiction   103

Venting anger does not resolve anger. It just leads to more venting.

The road to hell   105

Our intentions may be so good they gleam but they are not by themselves a remedy for anything.

Talking   107

For real communication (not pseudo-communication), two things must be present: honesty, yes, but humility most of all.

Three essential words   110

Yes. No. Maybe.

Listening   111

The sole and essential pre-condition for true listening is inner space.

Thin ice   113

The hoped-for right words turn out to be the wrong words; a situation we want to improve is made worse.

My story, my millstone   115

We step into our work when we step out of our story.

A lousy question   118

"What's the problem?"

Here are your options   120

Change the situation. Leave the situation.

Now   121

NOW is the perfect time because NOW is the only time.

A mild form of insanity   123

Complaining is so common most people regard it as perfectly normal.

Actions and reactions   125

Can you see how simple this is? How men of action do not make reality into a problem?

Let the past go   127

True forgiveness takes no effort at all.

Beliefs, opinions, principles   129

When we die, all of our opinions, belief systems and ideologies will die with us. They will cease to matter.

Your gift to the world   132

Your greatest gift to the world is not some-thing but no-thing.

Death   134

Every single day offers multiple and subtle opportunities to practice the fine art of a good death.

Breathe   136

Nothing exceeds the value or power of the breath. It is easily your most potent and reliable ally.

Meditation   139

What is the difference between meditation and living an ordinary human life? None at all, as far as I can see.

Last words   141

No muck, no flower. No anger, no peace.

Sources   143

Preface

This book owes its existence to the almost 1,000 men's groups I have been privileged to facilitate or co-facilitate since 1992. I began my career as a men's group facilitator in a state-of-the-art treatment facility (observation rooms, one-way mirrors, recording equipment) annexed to a high-security women's shelter in Windsor, Ontario, Canada. Three years later, I entered private practice under the umbrella of Men's Counselling Services, a non-profit agency providing group and individual counselling for men, with which I continue to be associated.

The most satisfying work I do is to work with men in groups. Men are more difficult to herd than cats, so getting a group of them together under any circumstances and for any reason feels like a huge achievement. On the basis of no clinical evidence whatsoever, I estimate that 30 percent of a man's inner work has been accomplished the moment he takes a seat in a circle of men he does not know. Not for nothing has courage been described as the first and greatest of all the virtues.

In terms of actual practice, my preference is to work with hetero-geneous rather than homogeneous groups. Homogeneous groups have a specific focus, e.g., support groups, rehabilitation groups, anger/depression groups, groups for the divorced and separated, court-mandated groups, bereavement groups, and so on. The risk in these groups is that the core treatment issue — depression, for example — will be amplified by virtue of the fact that every person in the group is manifesting the same problem. A heterogeneous group, on the other hand, is by definition multi-issue — all sorts of problems, all sorts of men. These groups mimic real life in that they offer a diverse array of presenting problems, perspectives and resources. In a high-functioning heterogeneous group, leadership is a shared responsibility, with each member being clear about his therapeutic task and open to feedback from other members.

***

Anger: A Message for Men is unavoidably and obviously exclusive. It is written specifically for men, by a man. The language is non-inclusive, the pronouns gender-specific, the references masculine. Still, I trust this "deficiency" will not be a disadvantage. In an important sense, women are my audience. If they do not read it, support its intention and validate its message by passing it on to the men in their lives, then its outreach will be severely restricted. I have been a counsellor for 17 years, and most of the men I have counselled have been referred to me, directly or indirectly, by women. So this "message for men" is also — and especially — for women.

***

If some further justification were required, I would say that this book acknowledges and respects the differences between men and women. At a basic level, it makes sense for men to meet with men, and to explore what they hold in common. That is the meaning of communication — something held in common. So when men gather, an essential precondition for communication has been met. It is present in the simple fact of their meeting.

Finally, there is an ease and naturalness among men that is not there when women are present. Men need and enjoy the company of other men. When this natural impulse is harnessed to self-inquiry, wonderful things can and do happen. My work has convinced me that a new and higher consciousness among men has begun to emerge, and that there is no turning back.

**

Life is not a straight line, and neither is this book. You may start at the beginning and read it straight through, but that is not necessary. Approach the contents however you want. Open it anywhere. Start from anywhere. Use what helps. Discard the rest. It is quite possible that the entire value of this book will be found in a single quotation.

**

There are no accidents: Life gives us what we need when we need it. I am immensely grateful to my friend and colleague Keith Fraser for 30 years of brotherhood. Without him, this small book would not be. I am grateful to my parents, Ray and the late Phyllis Ashford, for their love and generosity; to my "godfather" Richard Rohr (OFM) for his lion's heart and earthy spirituality, and to Eckhart Tolle and Dr. Jacob Liberman, for their wholly original work as harbingers of a new and arising consciousness. I also wish to thank Josh Baran for his wonderful book *365 Nirvana Here and Now* (recently reprinted as *The Dao of Now*), from which many of the quotations in this text were taken.

Introduction

Everything in life comes to you as a teacher.
Pay attention.
Learn quickly.
Old Cherokee woman to her grandson

Welcome to a little book on anger — a little book because anger does not merit a big one or a lot of words. It is just an emotion, a feeling, after all. No need to complicate what is really very simple.

I owe anger a debt of gratitude. Without anger, I would never have come into contact with the hundreds of extraordinary men whose honesty and humility have enriched my life. Anger, more than any other issue, is what brings men into my office. It is also what brought me back to myself.

Anger has been a great teacher for me. At first, I didn't recognize it as a teacher. But constant companion that it was, I finally realized it had to be more than just an enemy. Being with anger has given me depth and humility. It kept demanding my attention, saying, "Look at me! Look at me!" when my inclination was to look everywhere else.

As Gay Hendricks says, anger is a feeling that is best appreciated up close. Now, it just seems natural and right to maintain a close watch on my inner landscape. Self-observation happens on its own. I remember someone saying, when you have seen the face of the enemy, the war is over. And in a way that is true for me. The closer I got to my "teacher," the less distinct he became. So now, as I write this, I have a feeling of gratitude but no one to thank.

Perhaps this will be your experience, too.

Congratulations

You are the truth from foot to brow.
Now what else would you like to know?
Rumi

You say you want to deal with your anger? Congratulations! Your journey is under way and, in a sense, already complete. The recognition of one's dysfunction is a tremendous achievement. Alcoholics Anonymous has got this point exactly right — in order to get free of a problem, you have to know you have a problem. If you know your anger is self-imposed, if you long to be free of it, freedom is at hand.

Anger is but a small and superficial aspect of our being. If it was all of us, it would not ex-ist (stand out). Neither, if the whole world were yellow, would yellow stand out. Anger can exist only against the backdrop of its opposite: inner peace. And increasingly, it is the backdrop that beckons.

Even now you are far more peace than anger. You are standing or sitting, reading these few words, and everything is fine. Everything belongs. You are not angry. What you are is ready for freedom from the suffering that anger creates. Perhaps you are tired of the drama, of going around the same block over and over again, like Bill Murray in

Groundhog Day. Or maybe you have awakened to a crucial realization: "This is my life and I am 100 percent responsible for all of it."

This reaches the mature man as good news: It *is* my life, my creation, and I alone am responsible — not necessarily for what happens but for *how I respond to what happens.* After all, the root of responsible is response, and "ible" is a variant of "able." The capacity is mine, and no one but me is in charge of my response. In my experience, the men who get to full responsibility fastest are the ones who make the most significant therapeutic gains.

The good news now is that you have suffered enough; there is no need to suffer any more. This is not my message to you. This is the universal message of the world's great spiritual traditions. In that sense, it comes not from outside of you but from inside, from the depths of your own heart. Yes, you have suffered enough.

> *If one is sick of sickness, then one is not sick.*
> *The sage is not sick because he is sick of sickness.*
> *Therefore he is not sick.*
> **Lao Tsu**

The Mars/Venus thing

Some women hold the view that men are complicated. But from my side of the divide, men are not only *not* complicated, they are very simple. The male operates from one basic need: to feel respected. If a man feels respected, he will undertake anything and sacrifice everything. If he does not feel respected, despair and dissolution hover just around the corner.

In my limited view, the big difference between men and women is humility. When a male hears "humility," he conjures feelings of shame or embarrassment, of being exposed as inadequate or of failing to measure up. But that is not humility at all; it is the opposite of humility, a contraction of pride. Golda Meir was probably speaking to a male when she advised, "Don't be so humble; you're not that great."

The pride of the male is both self-conscious and slightly comical: We do not easily (or ever) ask for help. The reluctance of the male driver to ask for directions is not less true because it's a cliché. Are not GPS devices male-issue machinery? In telling contrast, women in crisis instinctively reach out for help from all available sources — counsellors, books, chat rooms, friends, colleagues, family members. And GPS devices, too, if it comes to that.

Men are idealists, and the first thing they idealize is themselves. If the ideal male (a mental concept cobbled together from cultural references) is strong, capable, unafraid and wise, so must they be. Of course, the idealized male is by definition the unrealized male; he does not exist.

The ideals men hold for themselves they also project onto the world. Many men believe devoutly in the existence of "the big picture." They in-corporate (take into themselves) a set of ideals or principles by which they are guided and supported. As naturally as a woman dies for a child, a man dies for a cause — for something bigger than himself. Corporations, politicians and religious ideologues know well this predisposition and routinely exploit it, jihad being one of the most current and grotesque examples. Men do not become soldiers to put bread on the table. They enlist in order to realize (to make real) a concept — liberty, democracy, freedom, a better world.

All of this big picture stuff can easily lead to an inflated sense of self. Richard Rohr warns that contemporary men are missing a vital instruction — namely, *you are not that important.* Without this wisdom, they are at high risk to imagine that life is all about them. The fruit of that delusion is a terrible restlessness, an endless striving for significance. But men are like all life forms — ephemera, briefly illuminated, here and gone:

As for man, his days are like grass; he flourishes like a flower of the field; for the wind passes over it, and it is gone, and its place knows it no more.
Psalm 103:15-16

I cannot imagine a greater correction for promiscuous self-regard than a long, slow walk through a cemetery. This is what all of our life stories are eventually reduced to, observes Eckhart Tolle — the dash between two dates on the face of a stone. And so concludes the drama of me: a mound of ash, a few bones, a memory trace. How can anyone regard himself as important?

Especially in our early years, men are generally unaware of the cycles of life. Women are innately attuned to these cycles — to expansion and contraction, ebb and flow, joy and sorrow, health and sickness, for better and for worse. Menstruation is one of the most basic cycles of all, and to men such an unfathomable mystery! Small wonder that women are more at ease with blood (and especially the loss of it) than men. Women may cry out during childbirth, but they do not go into shock, they do not faint.

Intimacy with life's cycles creates a different kind of knowing. Travellers to Jerusalem may visit an ancient cave located just west of the city. Thought to be a ritual immersion pool, it has associations with the ministry of John the Baptist. One of the intriguing features of this cave is the 28 stone steps leading to the underground pool. Now, a man might regard 28 steps as a construction convenience, an arbitrary number, but what woman could miss the deeper significance of 28, the obvious reference to lunar and menstrual cycles?

For everything there is a season and a time for every matter under heaven: a time to be born, and a time to die; a time to plant, and a time to pluck up what is planted: a time to kill, and a time to heal; a time to break down, and a time to build up; a time to weep, and a time to laugh; a time to mourn, and a time to dance; a time to cast away stones, and a time to gather stones together; a time to embrace, and a time to refrain from embracing; a time to seek, and a time to lose; a time to keep, and a time to cast away; a time to rend, and a time to sew; a time to keep silence, and a time to speak; a time to love, and a time to hate; a time for war, and a time for peace.

Ecclesiastes 3:1-8

Although a woman's way of knowing is not the same as a man's, there is wisdom and compassion in both ways. The things that matter — peace, joy, love — are genderless. One of the sure signs of a new and emerging consciousness is a blurring of gender differences. How else to explain the up-to-now improbable popularity of a performer like Antony Hegarty? A mainstream movie like *Brokeback Mountain*? The growing cultural allowance for same-sex parents?

Rites of initiation

It used to be that when boys reached puberty they were ritually separated from their mothers and families and brought deep into the wilderness to be instructed by tribal elders in the essentials of how to be a man. In North America, these rites of passage have pretty much vanished, with only trace elements to be found in a few religious observances (Bar Mitzvahs, for example) and First Nation ceremonies. Without elders or godfathers to take seriously the importance of inner work, today's young men have to figure it out on their own. Some do, most do not. And that is one of the painful realities of our time.

In a way, men's therapeutic groups are both a reclamation and restatement of the ancient traditions. Men's groups are completely countercultural. The emphasis of the prevailing culture is on the little "me," the self or ego. As a result, men become so personalized and individualized that they cannot access their own depth. Men at this stage of under-development are completely unaware of their shamanic power — that is, of the power that has traditionally been put at the service of a larger story than me and mine.

Men are capable of acts of amazing tenderness. Those who have been wounded by other men (including, to greater or lesser degrees, by their own fathers) can also be healed by men — and when that happens the healing is all the more powerful. I respect Oprah and much of what she does, but I am dubious that a female forum is the best place for men to name and weep over their wounds. Modesty and restraint are among the great virtues, but these qualities are generally absent in televised therapy sessions.

Nor does it feel right to me that men — especially men who have been in a destructive relationship with a woman — should in their grief and guilt seek out a woman to help them. Pierre Schaeffer, a musician and student of the great spiritual teacher G.I. Gurdjieff, enlarged on this point in an interview:

> *What Gurdjieff asked was that we not consider a woman as a dumpsite and that we not burden the love of a woman with all our existential problems — that we have the dignity, the modesty, and the strength to take these problems upon ourselves. Not to assume that everything can be solved by marriage. This is what Gurdjieff asked and it is still very poorly understood.*

Were the roles to be reversed, my view would be the same: Women do not need men to help them plumb their psyches. They are perfectly capable of solving their own problems. I say this as a husband of more than 30 years and as the father of two daughters. It is men who must learn to do for themselves what women have always done beautifully.

Primarily, men must investigate and take responsibility for their emotional lives, especially anger and fear. For as long as we fail to do this — and generally we do not do it until circumstances, life itself, forces us to do it — we will be loose cannons: reactionary, rash, prone to violence. Or we will "numb out," becoming remote and unconnected, abandoning author-ship (authority) of our lives.

The Quest

The search may begin with a restless feeling, as if one were being watched. One turns in all directions and sees nothing. Yet one senses that there is a source for this deep restlessness; and the path that leads there is not a path to a strange place, but the path home.
Peter Matthiessen

We are not whole, it seems — half of us is missing. Consider the yin and yang of creation, the tension between the polarities, the immutability of sexual attraction. All of these are written into life. They perplex, inspire, mystify and motivate us. The quest for our missing part, for ultimate union, would appear to be the point and purpose of life.

For the young man, the quest is typically outward-going and action-oriented. He leaves home, enters into a long-term relationship, pursues a career, raises children, invests in the myth of happily ever after. Later, in his middle years, it may happen that his attention shifts from the world of win/use/compete/succeed to an inner dimension that is less quantifiable and goal-oriented, more reflective, inquiring and fluid. A man in the midst of this shift is undergoing a transformation of consciousness. Many of the old certainties no longer apply. He may ask: Outside of my role, who am I? Why am I here? What is my purpose?

Generally, men in their teens and twenties have no need and no time for inner work, for the world of feeling and intuition. Their reference points are the usual suspects — sports heroes, business titans, tough guys. They embody what Richard Rohr calls the shallow masculine.

Tragically (and sometimes comically), many men remain in Rambo-mode for a lifetime, bellowing their opinions, telling it like it is to an ever-diminishing audience, "full of sound and fury, signifying nothing." At this level of development, the male has relatively little of lasting significance to give to others. It is not until men reach their 30s and 40s, when the cracks in the looking-good-game begin to appear, that the opportunity (and even the necessity) for a program of self-inquiry presents itself.

The road to the deep masculine goes through the heart — what depth psychologists call the feminine. We cannot skip the emotions and be real. That is the blessing of anger. This two-by-four of the emotional life is so blunt and powerful that it cannot be ignored. It demands our attention.

The shift from outer to inner is often precipitated by an experience of pain or loss — divorce(s), bankruptcy, ill health, depression. Mythologists call this the Fall — or, as psychology prefers, a mid-life crisis. By whatever label, the experience is real. The first response of the uninformed male is to reject the experience, to get angry about it. No one told him about the inevitability of the Fall, still less about what he most needed to know — how to fall gracefully.

Or, maybe someone did, but the male missed it. As Scott Peck points out in *The Road Less Travelled*, all the world's great religions are in essential agreement on one great truth: *To live is to suffer*. That message is a tough sell in a materialistic, consumer-driven and success-oriented culture. It is mostly unheard or unheeded.

The Fall

Humpty Dumpty sat on a wall.
Humpty Dumpty had a great fall.
All the king's horses and all the king's men
Couldn't put Humpty together again.

The first thing to know about this nursery rhyme is that Humpty Dumpty is not an egg, though he — unmistakably a he! — is illustrated that way in the children's anthologies. The second thing to know is that the Fall is a messy business. And the third is that outside agencies, even the biggest and most powerful ones, cannot un-ring the bell. The Fall represents an irreversible change, a radical re-ordering of our priorities, a transformation of life.

In the event of the Fall, be assured you will have what you need — which is nothing much. You are falling, after all. Awareness is the main thing. No one can pay attention for you. This is your experience. No one else can feel, allow or surrender to what is happening. It is happening to you. Therefore, trust yourself.

Finally, falling is not climbing, so you might as well relax as you tumble from the tower of achievement. There is no condition in life — not even falling — that can be improved upon by feeling tense. This is fundamental to the martial arts. Relax! Ultimately, power comes from expansion, not contraction. Let what must happen, happen.

The obvious application for men who suffer with anger is: Allow the emotion to be as it is. Do not impede this rough guest, or attempt to toss him angrily out of the house. Do not leave the house yourself. Engage this unruly visitor with your complete attention. Stand up and face him. Allow his wild energy to flow right through you. Novelist Henry Miller writes about being present to our lives in just this way:

> *Life moves on, whether we act as cowards or heroes. Life has no other discipline to impose, if we would but realize it, than to accept life unquestioningly. Everything we shut our eyes to, everything we run away from, everything we deny, denigrate or despise, serves to defeat us in the end. What seems nasty, painful, evil, can become a source of beauty, joy and strength, if faced with an open mind.*
>
> *Every moment is a golden one for him who has the vision to recognize it as such.*

Anger is temporary

The word "emotion" is derived from the Latin word for disturbance. Some disturbances are more pleasant than others — receiving unexpected presents, celebrating with friends, falling head over heels in love. Most, however, are exceedingly unpleasant — jealousy, fear, anger, grief. Whether unpleasant or pleasant, all emotions have temporariness in common.

The turbulence of anger can be compared to the waves whipped up on the lake by a strong wind. Like all disturbances, the condition is impermanent. It will blow for a while, then stop. Anger, too, is strictly a surface phenomenon, but because of its heavy, negative charge, we tend to overestimate its significance. A fathom below the surface, all is calm, quiet and still.

If the lake is considered in its wholeness, it is never *not* peaceful. It is simply too large and too vast to be contained or defined by a passing weather condition. In the same way, the sub-surface you, the real you, is immutably peaceful. There are passing disturbances — there always are — but deep down we are undisturbed by life's ups and downs. We are not unaware of them, of course, but the news of the day is seen for what it is — fleeting images on the screen of consciousness. The passing show is not us.

Nothing real can be threatened.
Nothing unreal exists.
A Course in Miracles

We lose our poise when we get lost in a feeling, when we invest an emotion with ultimate meaning. A loss of perspective is often expressed by catastrophic language, even on subjects as mundane as the weather: *What a dreadful day! Absolutely terrible! It couldn't be worse.*

Poise regained? When the weather is just the weather, sunny one day, cloudy the next, neither good nor bad. When our emotions are just our emotions, one day happy, the next day sad. When our deeper connection is to a state of being which is changeless and true.

Every emotion has imbedded within it the seed of its opposite. Happiness carries sadness, pleasure carries pain, success carries failure. Airline pilots articulate a life wisdom when they say "Prepare for some turbulence." You are at the top of your game? Everything perfect — the job, the family, the finances? It cannot last because life is inherently unstable and no condition prevails for long. So says a starkly simple Japanese poem about the bottom-heavy daruma doll:

Seven times down,
Eight times up,
Such is life!

We reconnect with what is lasting when we recognize what is passing. The "you" who watches an emotion go by is your wise owl, your wisdom source, your inner witness. Can you be as aware of the one who watches emotions as you are of the emotions? Can you be aware of awareness?

I am an angry man

No, you are not. You are a man in whom there is an emotion but you are not the emotion itself. A man who thinks he is a feeling is at the mercy of the feeling. He has temporarily lost himself.

In our natural state, we are *aware* of a feeling. We are a field of consciousness in which feelings come and go, rise and fall. As Toni Packer puts it, "Pure awareness is the essence of what we truly are. We are not the different states and feelings, moods and tempers succeeding one another. All of it comes and goes lightly, cloudlike, without leaving a trace, when thought doesn't identify with any of it."

A well-known parable describes how an orphaned lion cub is rescued and raised by sheep. The lion grows up thinking he is a sheep. He learns to bleat like a sheep, to eat grass instead of meat, and to seek his security in the middle of the flock. One day, an old lion happens by, sees the young lion and drags him off. The young lion kicks and screams, terrified that he is going to be eaten. Given his youth and strength he could have easily overpowered the old lion, but thinking like a sheep, this does not occur to him. The old lion takes him to a pond and directs him to look into the water. Upon seeing his reflection, the young lion "wakes up" to his real identity.

You are not an emotion. You are a lion. You are not what you feel. You are the awareness of a feeling. Beneath the emotion, surrounding it, in the silent space between it and the next emotion — there resides your true power, the source of creativity, courage and peace. Ultimately, only silence is vast enough to accommodate the reality of who you are:

The great teachings unanimously emphasize that all the peace, wisdom and joy in the universe are already within us; we don't have to gain, develop or attain them. Like a child standing in a beautiful park with his eyes shut tight, there is no need to imagine trees, flowers, deer, birds, and sky; we merely need to open our eyes and realize what is already here, who we already are — as soon as we stop pretending we're small and unholy.
Bo Lozoff

Nothing to fix

Anger is not a mechanical problem. It does not require fixing. It needs only to be observed, investigated, inquired into, accepted. Usually men need a reason to move from the circumference of life (my marriage, my money, my career, my kids) to the centre of life (who I am without a role). You have been activated, summoned to awareness, by anger. It was the only thing strong enough to get your attention. You have awakened from the dream of the unexamined life. An enemy would have let you sleep.

Your first task is to stop feeling angry about feeling angry. Your anger was inevitable. How can we know that? Because it happened. So the question is not "Why am I angry?" The question is "Now what?"

The key is to be who you are. If you are angry, then you are angry. Why make a problem out of a feeling? Why complicate things by declaring "I should not be angry"? To say that I do not want to be who I am, that I want to be like somebody else — well, this is what hypocrisy means. It represents an effort that cannot be sustained and is frankly unbelievable to everyone.

Throw open the doors of perception. See the anger. Does it have a colour? Feel the anger. Where in your body is the feeling most intense? Invite anger in. It is, after all, in already. One of two things will happen. You will either become anger and ransack the house, or you will become the watcher, the fair witness, the one who sees, feels and, most important of all, allows.

> *Can anger be overcome by effort, by various methods and techniques, by meditation and various forms of transforming "what is" into "what is not"? Now, suppose that instead of making an effort to transform anger into non-anger, you accepted or acknowledged that you are angry, what would happen then? You would be aware that you are angry, which is "what is", and knowing the stupidity of transforming "what is" into "what is not", would you still be angry? If instead of trying to overcome anger, modifying or changing it, you accepted it and looked at it, if you were completely aware of it, without condemning or justifying it, there would be an instantaneous change...*
> **J. Krishnamurti**

If everything else has failed, try this: Give up trying.

The power of observation

When anger arises, don't just do something — stand there. Simply pay attention. Be aware of the feeling. Your mind has a limited role to play. Once the feeling has been named ("I feel angry"), it is out of a job. The mind will rebel against this restriction. It will want to explain the feeling, or to make someone responsible. Ignore it. The mind has done its work. Be strict about this.

Feel the feeling. Anger can feel like a sickness. Its vibration is negative, viral, unpleasant. Let each in-breath take you deeper into the feeling. Let each out-breath release the feeling from your body. The more often you do this, the easier it gets.

Allow the feeling. Do not resist or judge it. Do not take it personally. Do the only thing you can do — surrender to what is. Assign no blame to others, neither bring any blame onto yourself. If you find yourself doing either of these things, know that the mind has climbed down the chimney and invited itself back into the process.

Anger will do everything possible to ensure that you do not relate to it in this way. It does not want to be studied, investigated or allowed. It wants you inside the ring as a featured performer, a combatant, not high in the bleachers watching the action.

Nothing deflates anger more quickly than when it is observed. Confirm for yourself how quickly anger abates whenever it is watched. It is almost as if anger is embarrassed to be seen. The closer your attention, the more unwavering your gaze, the more rapidly the feeling shrinks.

Watching anger changes everything. This is not a skill you need to develop; it is a natural ability, something innate and powerful. When you reconnect with your observing presence, you disconnect from anger. When you disconnect from anger, you reconnect with yourself.

Your observing presence *is* peace.

A feral boy

Let us imagine anger looks and acts like this: An adolescent boy raised by animals. No language. No ability to reason. No capacity for self-reflection. Trapped in the wild, now the subject of clinical study, he is terrified and full of rage.

The boy is on one side of a two-way glass partition, and you are on the other. A curtain parts, and the two of you briefly make eye contact through the glass. Suddenly, the kid goes completely berserk, leaping about, face contorted, hurling himself against the glass, excreting, howling, absolutely out of control.

You are sitting in your chair, on the other side of the glass, watching. You are relaxed, still, not reacting to this demonstration of wildness. You know any attempt to placate the boy would only prolong the outburst. You sit and watch, detached but not indifferent, alert and easy. You are certain of one thing: This can't last.

And it doesn't. The energy peaks, and then it is over. The shrieks subside into moans, the body deflates, seems almost to melt. A minute more and the boy sinks to the floor and curls into himself. He casts one last glance in your direction and then falls asleep.

For some men, this is how a burst of adrenalized anger truly feels —

powerful, primal and animalistic. They may have some mix of shame and embarrassment about this, wondering if they are freaks, as if they alone know what it feels like to play host to an emotion that is so dark, visceral and raw.

Like crossing the street

Be aware of anger as it happens. Witness it. Stay connected with the feeling in your body. Anger is a highly charged energy vibrating somewhere in the body — commonly in the chest as a concentrated tightness, as a pain in the gut, or a muscle contraction in the neck or back. Observe your desire to make it go away. Know that there is no "away." There is a feeling in the body. Do not judge it. Be a gracious host. Allow it to be as it is.

When you let it be, you let it go. Only make sure you let it go completely. Notice what remains when the feeling has gone, when every wisp and tendril has vanished. You are now in the region of the real you. You are now at peace. If anger has one true enemy, inner peace is it. To repeat: Be aware of your anger. Hold it in your consciousness. Let it be as it is.

No techniques, strategies or 12-step programs are required. Anger exists for no other reason than to be acknowledged. There is no need to do anything, only to notice everything. Anger is the emotional equivalent of a red light: Pay attention! Right now!

I could characterize nearly any spiritual practice as simply being: identify and stop, identify and stop, identify and stop. Identify the myriad forms of limitation and delusion we place upon ourselves, and muster the courage to stop each one. Little by little deep inside us, the diamond shines, the eyes open, the dawn rises, we become what we already are.

Bo Lozoff

You need curiosity, detachment and a willingness to observe this most insistent phenomenon. It helps if you can catch the feeling the moment it appears, if you can become immediately aware of its vibration in the body, and of the thoughts that generate it. Maintain your attention for as long as it takes. That is all. That is everything. Can you stop what you are doing and do that?

When you recognize the importance of paying attention, you *will* pay attention.

Control issues

Perhaps you have what others describe as "control issues." Maybe you acknowledge having them yourself. If you are, indeed, a controlling person, then anger has the keys to your house. Nothing in life can be controlled — at least not for long.

Controlling your anger is like putting a suit and tie on a wolverine. No one is really fooled by the suit. The wolverine remains a wolverine. Controlled anger is anger in its most unconvincing disguise. Sooner or later, it will leak out (as criticism, impatience, a poisoned silence) or burst out (as profanity or violence). Who can be surprised or disappointed when the inevitable happens?

The term "anger management" is misleading to the extent that management implies control. The phrase probably reflects our culture's over-valuation of business models. In the corporate world, problematic emotions are like underperforming employees — they just need to be managed better. Or, after a third negative performance appraisal, fired.

Some anger management programs include the suggestion that we make a list of our triggers and avoid them. This is a most dubious strategy given life's extravagant generosity with triggers. It could even be proposed that life itself is a trigger. A strategy that depends on an avoidance of life for its success is not going to work very well, or for very long.

We are not in control. It seems that all of life is set up to teach us that, and yet we persist in believing the opposite — believing that we can control what happens, control others, control how we feel and, at the end of all that controlling, somehow find freedom.

No doubt the exercise of control has some limited and short-term utility in the outer life — in emergency situations, for example. But in terms of the inner life, *control does not work*. And neither does its better-dressed cousin, Will Power, sorry to say.

The more we attempt to control our anger, the more we empower and prolong it. All non-acceptance achieves is some form of physical or psychological suffering. Many men require the experience of great suffering before they are able to finally relinquish the illusion of control.

What we resist persists.

St. Catherine of Sienna said of life that it's "Heaven all the way to heaven; hell all the way to hell." If control has not worked, then control will not work. Turn it around 180 degrees. Let it go. Let it be.

In men who are free (uncontrolled), emotions have a short shelf life. They appear and disappear very quickly. I once watched as a Zen monk, in the process of relating an incident that had taken place in the kitchen, cried and laughed in the space of about a minute and a half. When the emotions had passed, they were truly gone. Like a painting in the water, neither his tears nor his laughter had left a trace.

All that is really needed is for anger to be observed, recognized and allowed. Watching without interfering, permitting instead of resisting

—— this changes everything. It requires no skill or training to do this; it is a natural state of simple awareness *without mental commentary*, like watching a televised playoff with the sound turned off.

> *If you begin to understand what you are without trying to change it,*
> *then what you are undergoes a transformation.*
> **J. Krishnamurti**

The real problem

Yond Cassius has a lean and hungry look,
He thinks too much; such men are dangerous.
William Shakespeare *(Julius Caesar, Act 1, Scene 2)*

As a man, I observe, without irony or derogation, that the majority of men are mental. The head is our control tower; we have "thought" into existence the world in which we live, and we are paying the price for that in conflict and suffering. Thinking is not the unqualified positive that so many have for so long believed. For support of this contention, consider the state of the planet.

Eckhart Tolle says flatly that it is a matter of urgent necessity for humankind *to stop thinking*, and to access a deeper consciousness compared to which our mental processes are a mere triviality. The source of this counter-cultural remedy? Well, not the mind, that's for sure. The mind cannot distinguish between wisdom and mere cleverness. It insists that thought is wisdom and wisdom is thought and that the solution to our problems is a think tank away.

The fact is, anger comes from nowhere other than the mind. It has no objective reality. It is not "out there" in the world, nor is it inherent in events that happen or do not happen. It is purely subjective, a response in the body to a thought by the mind. It will either be projected outward in the form of blame or conflict, or "introjected" to some deeper place in the body, where it will continue to foment until it eventually manifests as a physical illness.

"The primary cause of unhappiness," says Tolle, "is never the situation but your thoughts about it."

Anger is a symptom. The mind is the problem.

No mind, no problem.
Seung Sahn

I have a right to be angry

Yes, you do, and no one is going to take that right away from you.

So, now that we have established your right to be angry about whatever it is you are angry about, what have we accomplished? We have established that someone or something other than you is responsible for how you feel.

It takes no special awareness to realize that there is no light at the end of this tunnel. Claiming the right to be angry is like claiming the right to bang your head against a concrete wall. The question is, why do something that is so obviously self-injurious? When the absurdity of anger is fully recognized, the need to justify it disappears. Imagine how good you will feel when you stop feeling angry. Let us not make this more complicated than it needs to be. You stop it when you drop it.

Unclench your fist. Let it go. Can it really be as easy and immediate as that? Absolutely. Compare the experience of dropping the red-hot coal with the experience of continuing to hold it. That was the Buddha's suggestion, so it seems that anger was not unknown to him — nor was how to be in its presence.

The four-car train to anger

Here is the predictable chronology by which anger is aroused. Now, just because the chronology is predictable does not mean it is slow to unfold. Anger is *the* most powerful negative emotion; it can shoot to the surface at warp speed. What reads like a sequence in time is actually the content of a single moment.

1) Something happens. You win $500 at the track. A bus runs over your foot. These are events or life situations. It could be anything. Life unrolls in all kinds of ways.

2) You think about what happened. Your mind interprets the event negatively or positively.

3) Your thought produces an emotion, a disturbance felt somewhere in the body. The emotion will be positive or negative depending on whether the thought was positive or negative. A negative thought cannot yield a positive emotion, nor a positive thought a negative emotion.

4) You act out the feeling. If the emotion is negative, you will behave negatively. If the emotion is positive, you will behave positively.

Most men come to counselling because of a pattern of negative behavior. But negative behaviour is not the problem — it is a symptom of a negative emotion. Neither is the negative emotion the problem — it is a symptom of a negative thought. Backed up as far as it can be, the culprit is revealed as a thought, a mental model of how things should be.

It is not enough to modify one's behavior. If all that changes is how we act, nothing changes. The only thing we have done is push the ice cube to the bottom of glass. The strategy of submerging anger cannot work on any level. The action itself is a lie.

The mind can trigger emotion even in the absence of an event, simply by recalling the past or imagining the future. If you are relaxing in the bathtub and you suddenly remember something "terrible" that happened two weeks ago, or worry that something "awful" might happen tomorrow, then you will experience either anger or fear, followed by a palpable constriction somewhere in the body. Objectively, there is absolutely nothing to fear — you are lying in the tub! Your thoughts, of course, lie elsewhere.

Thought and emotion are the Glimmer Twins. The one affirms and supports the other. Emotion does not challenge or contradict the mind; it is the ultimate yes-man, confirming what the mind has decided is true. Thought feeds emotion, and emotion feeds thought. The ancients had a symbol for this cycle — a snake swallowing its tail.

Nothing is either good or bad. It's thinking that makes it so.
William Shakespeare

Why am I angry?

According to *A Course in Miracles,* we are never upset for the reason we think. We think we are upset because of something that has happened. Not true. We are upset because something has happened that we think should not have happened. Life has run afoul of our mental models.

Can you see the difference? Can you feel how stressful it is to be at odds with reality?

Thinking that something should not have happened does nothing to change the fact that it *has* happened. It is our unwillingness to accept *what is* that creates anger. One cannot be in a negative relationship with reality and not be angry.

There is a hidden error in the question "Why am I angry?" — the presumption that you should not be angry. When you ask this question, not only are you at odds with the facts on the ground, you are at odds with yourself — a classic case of double jeopardy. But this is how the unobserved mind operates. It opposes reality, and then it opposes you. It kicks you in the backside coming and going.

When you are angry, acknowledge that you are angry. *I am angry.* Full stop. Accept that you are feeling angry; do not pass judgment on what you are feeling; do not wish for some other emotion; do not blame someone else for the fact of the feeling. Feel the anger as it moves through the body. Observe your thinking. You are aware of an experience. You don't need to change anything, only to be aware of everything. That's all. Seeing is doing.

Only humans think

Anger does not exist in the natural world. Do turtles get angry? Do owls or pheasants? Animals are born and die, feed and procreate, and they do it all without anger. Neither the trees nor the rivers nor the seasons know anything about anger. They change and flow with ease.

The reason there is no anger in the natural world is because nothing in the natural world thinks. Or needs to. Neither trees nor flowers do any thinking. The deer does not awaken and wonder, "What should I do today?" The turtle is not depressed. The robin does not resent the chickadee. The frog does not fuss over its many responsibilities.

When humans feel angry, we often become aware of an urge to get away from it all. The "all" that we want to get away from is the mind and its incessant thought-stream. In nature, *where there is neither thought nor any necessity for thought*, we reconnect to being-states of which the mind knows nothing: peace, joy, love.

This is surely why people love their pets, most especially their dogs and cats. These beautiful creatures provide a bridge to the natural world, to the world of no-thought. When a dog looks at his master, he is not judging the master, not comparing him to other masters, not worrying about whether supper will happen, not resentful because yesterday's walk was shorter than usual. The dog looks at the master with an absolute purity of being. If the dog could speak, it would say, "Isn't life great! Let's play!"

> At dawn Henry picked up his stick.
> It wasn't too short or too long.
> It wasn't too thick or too thin.
> Like the wilderness, it was the way it should be.
> Henry looked out over the world.
> And then descended into the rising mist.
> **Thomas Locker**

Repetitive thinking

The philosopher René Descartes had it half right when, after a lot of thinking, he said, "I think, therefore I am." He would have been closer to the mark had he said, "I think, therefore I am angry, confused, exhausted and going to bed."

Consider how the mind works. Observe it in action. Notice first of all its repetitiveness. It has been estimated that 90 percent of what we think we have thought before. What is the use in thinking the same thought, or series of thoughts, over and over again? Like a ruminating animal, the mind tends to chew its own cud.

The more we think, the less likely it is that we will produce an original thought. The unsupervised mind is an absolute hodge-podge of thought forms. Where in the jammed closet of the head is there room for love, beauty, creativity, spontaneity?

Imagine for a moment what life would be like if we thought only when we needed to think. Imagine the sheer spaciousness and ease we would feel, the energy we would have, the joy we would take in the mystery and majesty of life.

And calling to him a child, he put him in the midst of them, and said, "Truly, I say to you, unless you turn and become like children, you will never enter the kingdom of heaven."
Jesus

Where *is* the kingdom of heaven, this place of joy and peace? It is within you, say the world's most inspired teachers. It is a state of consciousness that cannot be created because it already is.

Imagine a beggar sitting on a crate by the side of the group asking for spare change. Inside the crate, completely unknown to him, is unimaginable wealth. He has no need of a pittance — he already has an abundance, more than he could spend in seven lifetimes!

Seek no more. There is no need. You are already complete.

Of this the mind knows nothing.

Negative thinking

No problem can be solved with the same consciousness that created it.
Einstein

In addition to being repetitive, most of what the mind thinks is negative. Watch your thoughts as often as it occurs to you to do so. See whether or not this is true for you.

Observe the expressions on the faces of the people on the subway, your colleagues at work, the cashier at the supermarket. If the automatic tendency of the mind is to think negative thoughts over and over again, it makes sense that many of us appear anxious, distracted, depressed or wishing we were somewhere else.

The mind defines itself in terms of what it opposes. *He is a bad person. I am a good person. She is wrong. I am right.* Without enemies, without something or someone to be against, what is a mind to do? The mind likes to be fully employed. Nothing so engages the mind as the presence of an enemy. Since negative thinking creates the most enemies fastest, the mind thinks negatively.

People and situations are habitually labeled — not by you but by your mind. Be aware of the label-like shorthand the mind employs whenever it thinks about the other, the opposition: jerk, stupid, incompetent, dishonest. Labels are a lazy man's reality; they obviate the trouble of looking beneath the surface. Prejudice could not survive without labels, nor could war or any other form of conflict.

The tendency to create an enemy out of people and situations puts us in an adversarial position with life. When life is our enemy, who will serve as our friend? Life reflects our thinking; it becomes for us what we think it to be. If life is our enemy, *we cannot but suffer* — and in the process of our suffering create suffering for others.

From flat tires to divorce, from sickness to death, from job loss to a failed furnace, yes, challenges arise continuously. But is every challenge bad? Is every loss or limitation a categorical wrong?

Here is the alternative: Not bad, not good. Maybe a flat tire is just a flat tire. If that's all it is, then you will do what is necessary to fix it. You will exhibit dignity and modesty as you undertake this task. You will not dramatize the situation. When the tire is flat, you fix the tire. Beautiful!

From Norman Vincent Peale (*The Power of Positive Thinking*) onward, much has been written and spoken about the possibility of changing how we think. In theory, this sounds like a great idea. But can we really rely on an internal "thought cop" to police the mind and to eliminate or reframe all negative thinking? I wonder if the exhortation to "think positively" may qualify as one of the worst pieces of advice we can offer, like telling an anxious person "Don't worry, be happy," or a depressed person to "Put on a happy face," or a child in a drug-infested neighbourhood to "Just say 'No.'"

Negative thinking cannot be resolved by the mind. Negative thinking *is* the mind. Asking the mind to solve a mind-made problem is like putting a kleptomaniac in charge of store security.

Compulsive thinking

Worse than its tendencies to repetitiveness and negativity is the sheer compulsivity of the mind. Even when there is no obvious benefit to be derived from thinking — when we eat, sleep, listen, love, create — still the thought train thunders relentlessly on, one thought after the other, with unstoppable momentum. Men whose sleep cycles have been compromised will often say, "I just can't stop thinking." The problem summarized!

A common experience is waking up shortly after falling asleep. Why? In a breathtaking assertion of independence, the mind has arbitrarily decided there is more thinking to do. And so, without any respect for the needs of the body, it wakes us up to do it.

Compulsive thinking means that we do not have a choice about whether we will think or not. We are compelled to do it, literally unable to stop. (As an experiment, try for 10 seconds not to think. What happens when the mind is threatened in this way? Is it not the case that you think more urgently?)

If we cannot stop thinking, we are addicted to thinking. Forget sugar: thinking is the first addiction. Secondary addictions (to drugs, illegal and otherwise, to television, alcohol, smoking, over-eating, pornography, etc.) are not just the offspring of our primary addiction, they are a way to cope with the suffering it causes. A drink or two, and our thinking slows. A few more, and it may stop altogether. Any activity that allows us to zone out or numb out provides a temporary respite from our addiction-in-chief.

Perhaps even the first part of Descartes' thesis was wrong. To say "I think" implies we have a choice about whether to think or not. But who would choose compulsive thinking if, indeed, we had a choice? Compulsive thinking is not something we do — it is something that is done to us. "Pay attention!" commands the mind at two o'clock in the morning when we are sound asleep. "Wake up! This is important. Think about this now!"

Where does anger originate? If we concede that most of what the mind thinks is repetitive, negative and compulsive — well, we have at the very least a likely suspect.

Life lesson: The mind is a mischief-maker. Your proper relationship to your mind is like that of an adult with responsibility for an unruly child. Do not invest the actions of the child with too much seriousness. It is just how an unruly child behaves.

A beautiful mind

Well, really, there is no such thing — not unless you regard the internal workings of a computer, or any other powerful and useful tool, as beautiful. Right now, I am using a computer to type these words. The computer is translating my thoughts into symbols. Excellent! But has the computer summoned the words or put them together? No. The computer, as powerful as it is, has all the limitations of any other tool. While it can be used to facilitate the process of creation, it is not in itself creative.

Minds and computers have a neutral value. We can use them to write poems or build bombs. The kind of creativity that heals and blesses comes *through* the mind but not *from* the mind. The creative act is an expression of the real you, the mysterious "I am" that is both the source of all wisdom and the essence of who you are. Your mind is a wonderful and powerful tool, but it is not more than that. We most truly appreciate the beauty of a sunset when the mind is silent.

You have a mind, but you are not your mind. Your mind is not beautiful. You are beautiful. The mind is most properly used to deal with day-to-day matters: to plan a trip, order a meal, purchase a car. Then, after the job is done, it is set aside. Pick it up. Put it down. That is the proper use of the mind.

The mind was never designed to be "on" all the time, any more than a car was designed never to be turned off. Minds that are never off eventually become dysfunctional. Today, we have clinical terms to describe the mind without an off switch: attention deficit disorder, hyperactivity, bi-polar disorder, schizophrenia.

The school systems I am familiar with say they are teaching our children to think. Our children do not need help with thinking. What they need is the ability to be alert and conscious *without* thinking.

Let the mind be compared to a top-of-the-line cordless drill — 24 volts, reversible, variable speed, adjustable clutch — absolutely the best drill money can buy. Three things to know before you buy this drill: First, it can do a lot of things, but it cannot do everything. Second, it should be off more than it is on. And third, if it is the only tool you have, you are pretty much up the creek project-wise.

To maintain the mind at optimal efficiency, rest it more than you use it; use it only when required; apply it to practical matters affecting your everyday life situation. One caveat: If you follow this prescription you run the risk of sainthood, the dual essence of which is simplicity and tranquility.

I turn over my little omelet in the frying pan for the love of God. When it is done, if I have nothing to do, I bow down to the ground and adore God from whom has come the grace to make it. Then I straighten up more contented than a king. When there is nothing more that I can do, it is enough to pick up a straw from the floor for the love of God.
Brother Lawrence

When we use the mind, we bless the planet. When the mind uses us, we add to the madness that threatens our survival as a species. The solution to the challenges we face, whether local or global, will come not from more thinking but from a deeper level of awareness. And, increasingly, there are signs that a great shift has begun. Many people speak of this as an awakening — an awakening out of thought and into consciousness.

> ...we are coming out of a kind of sickness here in the West, a sickness in the way in which we have overthought, the way in which we have been intellectually way ahead of our hearts' and bodies' wisdom. We're just learning how to quiet down a bit, and get it all together, which means that people who are trying to work with intellect as their primary yoga are dealing with a very hot fire.
>
> **Ram Dass**

Good news

You are not the mind. It is axiomatic that the perceiver [you] cannot be the perceived [the mind]. You can perceive your body; therefore, you are not the body. You can perceive your thoughts; therefore, you are not the mind. That which cannot be perceived or conceived is what you ARE.
Ramesh S. Balsekar

Some men have a curious response to the notion that it is possible to be fully awake and at the same time not thinking. *You're saying I can stop thinking? C'mon!* Sometimes this strikes them as so absurd they burst out laughing.

In one sense, they are right. Thinking cannot be stopped any more than anger can be stopped. But thoughts can be *observed* in precisely the same way that feelings can be observed, and with the same result.

When we bring the power of attention to our thinking, when we begin to consciously observe our thoughts, our thought stream immediately slows. The momentum of the mind depends on the degree to which we are identified with it. Be aware that the mind is very clever at what it takes to hook you in, to keep you thinking. It knows what works.

The unobserved mind develops a tremendous sense of self-importance. But it is an unclothed emperor, as your inner witness will confirm. How important, after all, is any thought that begins and ends in the mind? Can you recall last year's blue-ribbon thought? How about your most essential thought from yesterday, or an hour ago? They are mist on the lake, but in the moment of their arising they pretend to be so important. All of them do that. The mind does not discriminate in the assigning of importance.

In the moment that we step out of our thoughts and begin to watch them, we cut the lifeline of compulsive, repetitive thinking. A thought watched becomes shy and suddenly modest. And, if we watch closely enough — if we are, in Tolle's memorable simile, like a cat watching a mouse hole — thoughts...just...stop.

If you wait until you are in the middle of a "thought storm" to observe your thoughts, this task becomes more difficult. Practice watching your thoughts at low-stress points during your everyday activities. As you do this, you may notice that your thinking becomes less urgent, your thoughts less crowded. As you proceed, you may notice gaps between your thoughts — small spaces when you are awake and conscious but not thinking. Awareness of gaps, silence, empty space — these are signs of your arising consciousness. The era of the unsupervised mind is coming to a close.

Fear

In my experience, the majority of men who present themselves for counselling do so because of anger. It is perhaps the easiest of all the emotions for a man to own — or be owned by. In many cases, though, anger serves as a point of entry to an emotion more difficult to acknowledge: fear.

Counter-phobic fear impersonates anger. It looks like what it is not: fearless. At its most extreme, counter-phobic fear manifests as violence, foul language, homophobia and ultra-masculine behaviours. It is hyper-vigilant, sees enemies everywhere, sleeps with one eye open.

In its more moderate expression, counter-phobic fear can look like virtue, being prudent, cautious, risk-averse and concerned (often excessively so) about the future. Most repeated question: What can go wrong? Most immutable law: Murphy's. Life work: Prepare for the worst.

Fearful men are often conventional and rule-bound, though they would prefer not to be described in those terms. They tend to be sensitive to any kind of deviance from group norms, regarding as self-centered or traitorous those who do not conform to the rules the culture or the group has established to preserve itself.

Fearful men seek safety in numbers. They tend to be over-represented in organizations and institutions: academe, the military, the Mafia, the government, the judiciary, law enforcement, professional sports, big business. In these settings, fear wears a uniform, and long service is rewarded with a watch.

Counter-phobic men regard loyalty to the group as the highest good; its opposite, disloyalty, the most unforgiveable of sins. In fear-based organizations, the least plausible internal policies are those affording protection to whistle blowers. The truth is the system serves the system, and everybody hates a rat.

Frequently heard: "The rules are the rules — I didn't write them." "There is no 'I' in team." "What's the worst case scenario?" "Talk to my supervisor."

Men whose fear is unnamed and unrecognized will often go to great lengths to demonstrate that they are not afraid. They will step up, volunteer first, participate in extreme sports, take foolish risks. Of course, men who are truly without fear cannot be troubled to prove it. They are deferential, quiet, dignified. Why would they carry a weapon?

Only men of great courage can look fear in the face. When that happens, fear sinks to its knees, and true courage is realized. Great fear and great courage are two sides of the same coin. The most fearful men are potentially the most courageous. But until their fear is named, observed and allowed, they remain blind to their gift.

How many times does the Bible tell us to "Fear not." According to the movie *Facing the Giants*, 365 times. Once for every day of the year.

So you mustn't be frightened...if a sadness rises in front of you, larger than any you have ever seen; if an anxiety, like light and cloud-shadows, moves over your hands and over everything you do. You must realize that something is happening to you, that life has not forgotten you, that it holds you in its hand and will not let you fall. Why do you want to shut out of your life any uneasiness, any misery, any depression, since after all you don't know what work these conditions are doing inside of you?

Rainer Maria Rilke

"You" language

What he said: "When somebody cuts you off, you automatically get mad. You know?"

What he meant: "When somebody cuts me off, I automatically get mad. Am I clear?"

Fear and "you" language go together. "You" language is a reflection of the safety-in-numbers belief. It is an unconscious attempt to conscript the listener, to off-load the burden of my experience so that I will feel less alone and more supported. People who listen long enough to someone talking "you" language may become fatigued and distracted without knowing why. The conscious recovery of "I" language does two things: It restores clarity and power to the speaker; it gives space and freedom to the listener.

Restraint

In caring for others and serving heaven,
There is nothing like using restraint.
Restraint begins with giving up one's own ideas.
Lao Tsu

To identify with a feeling is to fall for an illusion. The real you is the opposite of an emotion — you are the field of awareness in which emotions appear and disappear. When you feel angry, the best and most you can say is, I am feeling angry. Full stop.

It sounds simple. It *is* simple. The challenge is not to say more than that. Rarely, in my experience, does "I feel angry" stand alone. And yet the truth requires no varnishing. There is an incredible dynamism in the simple confession of anger.

"I feel angry" also describes your immediate task: to feel angry. Immature men have difficulty accepting "I feel angry" as a job description. They want something done or someone punished. But action on the basis of anger is always wrong action. Before acting or speaking, feel the feeling. When you make it right on the inside, the right action arises by itself.

Do you sometimes sense that you do not have the attention of the person you are speaking to? Do you often feel unheard or misunderstood? You may be using too many words. So simplify. Say how you feel. That alone will bring everyone to attention.

The most beautiful word in the English language is restraint. Fewer words are better. Say more with less. As a Zen master might say, "Cut the crap."

Conscious suffering

To give up trying does not mean falling asleep or tuning out. It requires steadfast alertness to watch and stay with any negative emotion. Anger would much prefer that you have a drink, start an argument or turn on the television. The good news is that once your inner witness has been initiated, the canary is out of the cage. Self-observation becomes easier and more frequent until it seems to happen by itself. (Of course, it has been happening by itself all along.) Ultimately, you are not just free of anger — you are free, period.

Upon a soul absolutely free
from thoughts and emotions,
even the tiger has no room
to insert its fierce claws.
Zen poem

Nothing burns up anger more quickly than your willingness to bear it, to suffer it consciously, to watch, feel and allow it to be. Each time you experience it in this way, your capacity for anger is diminished, and your capacity for peace enhanced.

Make sure you do not turn anger into a story. Anger loves to be legitimized by a story. If you find yourself constructing a story (*She did this to me...*), stop it and drop it. Anger is just a feeling. It has no story any more than a cloud has a story. Nor is there anything personal in anger. It is not even about you. Anger is a life-form — in order to survive, it needs a host. You do not need anger. Anger needs you.

The moment anger enters your field of awareness, give it your full attention. Any delay gives anger a chance to establish itself. Mature men pay attention to the smallest disturbances. Why? Because they are naturally watchful and nothing escapes their notice. They also know from experience that small things, ignored or unattended to, can become big things. Why spend energy unnecessarily?

Paying attention to anger is the opposite of lifting weights. If you are exerting force, you are doing it wrong. Men who use exercise instead of awareness to deal with anger take note: aggressive exercise does not, in fact, diminish anger; it serves only to legitimize its existence in your body. Anger cannot be transferred to a punching bag. At the end of 15 minutes, you will feel utterly exhausted — but you will still be angry; indeed, depending on what you were thinking about while you were working the bag, your anger may have swollen.

Against the backdrop of your simple awareness, the bizarre behavior of what Buddhists call "monkey mind" will be on full display. That is to be expected. The noise in the head and the feeling in the body are as intimately related as conjoined twins. Pay attention to your "loudest" thought. It will surely be a negative one, and it will catastrophize everything. The moment you notice that alpha male thought, Byron Katie invites you to ask four questions:

1) Is the thought true?

2) Can you absolutely know it's true?

3) How do you react when you believe that thought?

4) Who would you be without it?

These are not "monkey mind" questions; they are "no mind" questions. They come from outside the cage.

Past, present, future

I have realized that the past and future are real illusions, that they exist in the present, which is what there is and all there is.
Alan Watts

For all the time we spend thinking about the past, we could be forgiven for believing that it actually exists. But, of course, the past does not exist, except as a present-moment thought. We cannot see, touch or change the past. If the past did exist, we could go there and fix it.

The future does not exist either, except — again — as a present-moment thought. This also is beyond dispute. You will never be in the future. No one has ever lived in the future, and no one ever will. Are we off the hook, then, in terms of planning, setting goals, saving money, booking a flight? Not at all. Life has its necessities, including the application of a certain kind of practical wisdom. Be aware, though, that when we plan for the future, we do it now. And when the future does arrive, it arrives as the Now.

No past,
No future.
Open mind,
Open heart.
Complete attention,
No reservations.
That's all.
Scott Morrison

My past is full of problems

Not so. Any problems you may have are in the present. It is technically impossible to have a problem in the past. If a problem is truly in the past, then you do not have a problem.

This is bad news for the ego, or false self, which would love to undertake a forensic analysis of Me and My Story. Ultimately, though, long-term analysis is an exercise without an end point. The deeper we go, the more there is to remember, regret and reflect on. Unless the process is terminated by sheer fatigue (paralysis by analysis) or suspended due to economic limitation, the study of me and my story can easily turn into a book of a thousand pages. And after that, what?

If we look for a solution to our pain in the past, we look in vain. It is not there. Would you look for a stock market tip in last week's newspaper? What is not now does not exist.

Anger happens in the only place it could happen — in the present tense. We deal with it experientially, not theoretically. We meet it now, in our flesh and blood, or not at all.

...Once you begin to deal with a person's whole case history, trying to make it relevant to the present, the person begins to feel that

he has no escape, that his situation is hopeless, because he cannot undo his past. He feels trapped by his past with no way out. This kind of treatment is extremely unskilled. It is destructive because it hinders involvement with the creative aspect of what is happening now, what is here, right now...

We must simplify rather than complicate the problem with theories of any kind. The situation of newness, this very moment, contains whole case histories and future determinations. Everything is right here, so we do not have to go any further than this to prove who we were or are or might be. As soon as we try to unravel the past, then we are involved with ambition and struggle in the present, not being able to accept the present moment as it is. It is very cowardly.

Chögyam Trungpa

Q & A

Q: *Aren't past and future just as real, sometimes even more real than the present? After all, the past determines who we are as well as how we perceive and behave in the present. And our future goals determine which actions we take in the present.*

A: *You haven't yet grasped the essence of what I am saying because you are trying to understand it mentally. The mind cannot understand this. Only you can. Please just listen. Have you ever experienced, done, thought, or felt anything outside the Now? Do you think you ever will? Is it possible for anything to happen or be outside the Now? The answer is obvious, is it not? Nothing ever happened in the past; it happened in the Now. Nothing will ever happen in the future; it will happen in the Now.*

What you think of as past is a memory trace, stored in the mind, of a former Now. When you remember the past, you reactivate a memory trace — and you do so now. The future is an imagined Now, a projection of the mind. When the future comes, it comes as the Now. When you think about the future, you do it now. Past and future obviously have no reality of their own. Just as the moon has no light of its own, but can only reflect the light of the sun, so are the past and future only pale reflections of the light, power, and reality of the eternal present.

Eckhart Tolle

The mind without a master

If you observe the activity of the mind, you will notice it is mostly about the past or the future. You may also become aware that you have a default setting to one or the other of these mind-created dimensions — that is, you will habitually think more often about past than future, or vice versa. Not that it matters, because outside of our mental imaginings, neither past nor future exist.

If you are seeking peace, compulsively thinking about past or future will not achieve it. Rage, anger, guilt, resentment and depression are emotions typically associated with thoughts about the past. Fear, worry, anxiety, tension and stress are usually related to a mind preoccupied with thoughts about the future.

Let's get busy!
Arsenio Hall

A most curious thing: The monkey mind is hyperactively busy in the dimensions that are unreal, past and future, where life does not happen. By contrast, the mind gives almost none of its attention to the present, to the one dimension that is real, where life actually happens.

This tells us two things: First, the mind loves to be busy. Second, the mind finds the present to be insufficiently stimulating. The present moment is always pretty simple. Right now, for example, I am sitting in a chair. What are you doing? The more rooted we are in the present moment, the more we see how quietly it operates, and how it has a way of taking care of itself.

In a true emergency, you will notice that the mind darts under the bed, covers its eyes and pretends it does not exist. It literally has nothing to contribute. Men who have gone through near-death experiences recall a feeling of ineffable calm. In the absence of thought, clarity and peace prevail. If something can be done to avert tragedy or death, it happens by itself, without thinking. In those experiences, an intelligence arises to which the problem-solving mind cannot be compared.

A mind that has been feverishly employed thinking about the past and the future develops a tremendous sense of self-importance. Depth psychologists call the inflation of this little self the ego. The ego's playgrounds are past and future. So much to think about! A shift to the present displeases the ego because the present lacks complexity.

Confirm for yourself that the Here and Now is essentially a problem-free zone. Of course, challenges arise from time to time, and the mind is quick to call them "problems." But are they really? Things come up and you deal with them. Where is the problem in that?

One of the most famous (and widely parodied) sculptures is Rodin's "The Thinker." It has for more than a century served as a paragon of intellectual activity. But, really, who can find any inspiration in this strange and unhappy-looking figure? Historians say the sculptor intended his massive work to represent the poet Dante in contemplation of "The Gates of Hell." He did what he set out to do by sculpting a man lost in thought.

No matter what the mind says, life is simple if life is now. Where is the complexity in what you are doing at this very moment?

Do not look back. And do not dream about the future, either. It will neither give you back the past, nor satisfy your other daydreams. Your duty, your reward — your destiny — are here and now.
Dag Hammarskjöld

Mind your own business

Byron Katie says there are three kinds of business: my business, your business and God's business. Observe your mind, and you will notice how much of its thinking is related to businesses other than our own. This is the cause of enormous suffering — when we step out of our business and into someone else's, presuming to know what must be fixed, improved or renovated.

We maintain our men's groups as "advice-free zones." Of course, there are lots of situations inside and outside of group when it is entirely legitimate to ask someone for advice, but unsolicited advice is an entirely different matter. Unsolicited advice is an act of aggression disguised as friendly concern. When you deconstruct unsolicited advice, some form of hostility is usually revealed. *You should do it this way! Listen to me! Do what I tell you! Are you so stupid that you can't see what I am saying is true?*

The giver of unsolicited advice enters before knocking; he jumps uninvited into the middle of someone else's business. Obviously, my "benefactor" has poor judgment and worse manners. Therefore, let him address his own liabilities before he concerns himself with mine.

On the inner level, when a thought arises, take it as an opportunity to ask yourself: Whose business am I in with this thought? If the answer turns out to be "God's business" or "someone else's business," get out of business.

Life gets very simple very fast when we tend to our own business. My business is what I am doing at this moment. Perhaps I am walking from one room to another, or making a cup of coffee, or picking up the telephone. These small actions are my business. If I am truly and totally in my business, I am performing each action with infinite care and close attention.

When walking just walk,
When sitting just sit,
Above all, don't wobble.
Yun-men

Don't wobble? Don't leave your business.

I pity the fool

Perhaps you've had the experience — on screen at the movies, or perhaps in real life — of watching someone who is so identified with their anger that they surrender their poise. They scream and howl, kick and punch, twitch and jerk. Faces redden, veins throb, fists clench. Respirations become rapid and shallow, the cardiac load obviously immense. One young man told me how in this state he could feel the hair on the back of his neck literally stand up. Individuals in this state of red-zone rage appear to be operating on the whim of a drunken puppeteer. And, in a sense, they are. If the condition were not potentially dangerous, even life-threatening, the performance would be hilarious.

This is an extreme expression of male anger — it represents a near-complete loss of self-awareness and is one of the reasons why men with less virulent manifestations are sometimes reluctant to ask for help. They are embarrassed to be identified with it. *Look, I'm not one of those guys who froth at the mouth...*

In a sense, it is simpler if the problem *is* red-zone rage. There is no mistaking exploding rage, which almost always comes attached to at least one very negative consequence. Red-zone rage is what happens when all the ammo explodes. Men who suffer anger this big don't need to grope around for words to describe their symptoms.

Controlled or repressed anger is a trickier bit of business. This kind of anger is more chronic than volcanic, more controlled than uncontrolled. It may also, in certain contexts, attract approval and reward. Perfectionism, for example. Or workaholism. Or competitiveness. Or naked ambition. Aren't these good things? Doesn't Donald Trump celebrate them?

Insight can be difficult when you are being applauded for living out the energy that's killing you.

Do sweat the small stuff

Much more common than red-zone rage is baby anger, the kind of anger that most men are completely unaware of. It is a term I have coined to describe anger in one of its most nascent, underdeveloped forms — boredom (yes, boredom), irritation, frustration, resentment.

And impatience, of course. The impatient man rarely takes note of his impatience, nor would he welcome hearing it called anger. Angry? Of course not. Just in a hurry, dammit, trying to get the job done. If he knew anything at all about baby anger, he might recognize hurry as a form of it.

Children unfailingly notice anger. They may not feel safe enough to name it, but they know how they feel when they are around it. If you have been "patiently" explaining something to a child, and shortly afterward you overhear the child asking, "Mummy, why is Daddy so angry?" you are being called to attention. A teacher — younger, smaller and less educated than you — is on the scene. Like all great teachers, the first thing he does is put a question on the table for which there is no answer.

If you cannot pay attention to, and take seriously, anger in its smallest forms, the likelihood of your being able to deal with big anger is pretty close to zero. If, however, you learn the lessons of baby anger, it is highly unlikely that you will ever need to deal with teenage- or adult-sized anger. All anger begins with baby anger. It is easy to know how someone will deal with big stuff, should the need arise. Look at how he deals with small stuff.

And, in fact, is not most of life small stuff? Take right now, for example. You are sitting or standing and you are reading these words. That's all. In another moment, you will be doing something else — maybe walking to the door, or getting into the car. Since most of life is small stuff, why not pay attention to it? Why not be present? What are you missing while you wait for something more important to come along?

The next time you are doing something absolutely ordinary, or even better, the next time you are doing something absolutely necessary, such as pissing, or making love, or shaving, or washing the dishes or the baby or yourself or the room, say to yourself:
"So it's all come to this."
Lew Welch

We are completely revealed in the smallest action. If you are afflicted with impatience, you will pick up a coffee cup *impatiently*. You will drive the car *impatiently*. You will stand in line *impatiently*. In a myriad of ways, mostly invisible to you, your anger will leak out of you. And on to others. Pretty soon, your whole world is drowning.

Life lesson: The way you do *anything* is the way you do *everything*.

A true man of no rank

Zen master Lin-chi used the phrase "true man of no rank" to describe the evolved male. So who in the third millennium is this person? Well, in the first place, he has

...immense courage and self-possession. Such a man has life for others and knows it. He does not need to push, intimidate, or play the power games common to other men because he possesses his power with surety and calm self-confidence. He is not opinionated or arrogant but he knows. He is not needy or bothered by status symbols because he is. He does not need monogrammed briefcases and underwear, his identity is settled and secure — and within. He possesses his soul and does not give it lightly to corporations, armies, nation-states or the acceptable collective thinking.
Richard Rohr

The true man of no rank knows himself from the inside out. He has been taught about anger; he knows from his own experience that the only way around it is through it. He learned this the hard way because there is no easy way, and ultimately every true man must do the work on himself, by himself.

Even so, a good teacher can be indispensable, as Lin-chi assuredly was. Sometimes, though, it is hard to recognize a good teacher, so here are a few tips:

First, a good teacher will almost certainly direct your attention inside of yourself — because that is where the answer to your question is. If you try to talk to him about how awful someone is, or how your wife or your parents don't understand you, or how your life is full of problems, he may tell you to stop wasting his time.

Second, a good teacher will express relatively little curiosity about the story of your life. If you insist on telling it to him, you may notice that at some point during the recitation he will start to smile. He is not making fun of you. He just cannot take your story with undue seriousness. When he looks at you, he sees who you are beneath the ego's storyline. He knows you are wonderful. Compared to your breadth and depth, what you are saying about yourself may strike him as utterly trivial.

Third, a good teacher may be disguised as a bad experience, e.g., as an encounter with pain, rejection, humiliation or loss. When one of these "teachers" appears, Jesus' advice was "Rejoice!" Lao Tsu said the same: "Accept disgrace willingly."

Does anybody do this? Are not people who rejoice in the middle of catastrophe called fools, or worse?

Personality

We tend to make judgments about people on the basis of their personality. A person with a pleasing personality is a good person. One with a displeasing personality is a bad person. If somebody is said to have lots of personality, it is generally taken as a compliment.

Let us be clear, however, about what personality actually means. It derives from the Latin word *persona*, for mask. By definition, a mask is fixed, immoveable, non-spontaneous, a sort of stock character in a play called "Life."

Personality begins to develop early in life, sometime around the age of three, and is not subject to change. It is not a bad thing to have a personality; in a conflicted and warring world, it acts as a sort of buffer, as insulation for the psyche. But it is not to be confused with who we are. The personality, or ego, is merely our game face, a sort of image we present to the world, behind which the true self resides.

Unfortunately, some of us are so completely identified with the one-dimensional personality (also called the false self) that we are unaware of what lies behind the mask (also called the true self). The personality is a form of conditioning, a litany of behaviours, of likes and dislikes. What we call personality is entirely a creation of the mind.

The false self is who we *think* we are.

The personality, which has security and pleasure as its aims, cannot be happy. Pursuing pleasure or safety will entail covering up any unpleasant or frightening truths. This automatically closes Joy. For Joy is the radiance of the heart when Truth is appreciated.
A.H. Almaas

One of anger's faces

I know of nothing more difficult than knowing who you are, and then having the courage to share the reasons for the catastrophe of your character with the world.
William Glass

According to an ancient Sufi teaching, anger expresses itself in nine different ways — that is, through nine different personality types. Each of these personae features a cluster of conditioned, unconscious behaviors. One of the nine types is known as the Perfectionist. His aliases include Critic, Judge, Teacher, Preacher, Paragon. This is a man whose anger is "dressed up" to look like a virtue. And what is that virtue? Being right, perfect and clean. Being on time and organized. Being honest, conscientious and responsible. And most of all, being a hard worker. See if you can recognize aspects of your (or another's) modus operandi in the following wood cut:

A high-energy, high-achieving "good boy." No capacity for unproductive play. Type A. Lives to work, works to live, relaxes by working. Enjoys being noticed for working hard.

The Dean of Clean. Hair groomed, beard trimmed, hands washed, nails clipped, cuticles cut.

Preferred appliance: the vacuum cleaner. Garage spotless, tools aligned, motorcycle/car/truck buffed, waxed, gleaming. Weed-free lawn cut on the diagonal. Everything in its place. Prefers not to lend things. Enthusiastic recycler.

Early riser, needs no alarm clock, hits the ground running. A human version of the EverReady bunny.

In childhood, preferred company of older children. A miniature adult. Well-mannered, trustworthy. Not observed spitting, swearing, stealing, talking back. Approved of by other parents.

As an adult, responsible, conscientious, driven. An achiever. Works to high standards, low tolerance for error. Never satisfied, critical of self and others, frequently feels guilty.

Determined, goal-oriented, mouth set in straight line. Frown lines appear early. Could not tell a funny story if a million dollars was at stake. No time for frivolity. Cannot understand why others are laughing. Resents suggestion he is humour-impaired.

Honest, moral, consumed with issues of fairness. Appreciated by supervisors for punctuality, observance of protocol, workaholic tendencies. Natural teacher, instructor, mentor, coach, referee. Excels in positions requiring attention to detail.

Only one right way to do things — his way, right away. No need for blueprints, instruction manuals. Knows immediately the best way to do everything.

Idealistic and moral. Tendency to lecture. Critical, judgmental, self-righteous. Jabbing, stabbing forefinger points out other people's mistakes. Repressed anger leaks out as impatience. Muscle tension in jaw, neck and back.

No slight forgotten, forgiven or passed over. Stuffs his anger. Denies being angry. Good boys not allowed to be angry.

Square face, blunt features, well-developed forearms. Strong, low centre of gravity. Good distance vision, acute olfactory sense. Warm hands/feet.

Anal-retentive — literally. Health issues related to the gut, intestinal tract, elimination. Takes antacids to combat reflux. Experiences most of life as indigestible.

Always talking and explaining things. Cannot be diverted from what needs to be changed, corrected, improved on. Extremely picky. Operates on a kind of automatic over-focus. Sees in an instant how things could be, should be, must be. Makes molehills into mountains.

Often disappointed in relationships. Something wrong with everything. Looks for perfection. Can't find it. Feels resentful.

Favourite words: have to, got to, must, should. Inner voice speaks in tones of praise-stingy parent: "Do it better! Work harder! Grow up!" As a child, concluded love was a reward for being perfect, working hard, doing it right.

Finds peace in nature, relates well to animals. Likely to own a dog, tend a garden, keep house plants.

Basic tension created by the burden of unexpressed anger.

Life "work": To lighten up.

No wax

Ring the bells that still can ring
Forget your perfect offering.
There is a crack in everything
That's how the light gets in.
Leonard Cohen

The virtue shared by men who make the fastest progress in counselling is sincerity. They have no energy left for polishing the apple. They are sick and tired of suffering, and they see plainly that the common denominator in their last three failed relationships was, well, "me." There is so much sincerity in "me" and so little in "It takes two to tango."

The word "sincere" comes from two Latin words meaning "without wax." It is widely believed that Roman craftsmen would wax their creations to conceal imperfections, the same way we use wax today to hide scratches on our cars. By this definition, a sincere man is un-waxed. His imperfections, flaws, cracks, weaknesses — the full spectrum of his imperfect humanity — are on display.

The best candidates for counselling are men in their thirties and forties. At that age and stage of life, men have cracks. As a result, they have access to the inside of themselves. Un-cracked men have no way in, no in-sight. That is why in the ancient Zen tradition, men needed to be older than 35 before they could undertake the spiritual disciplines of monastic life.

In the first part of life, men are too busy building their towers — competing, achieving, proving, climbing, winning. Ultimately, though, there comes a point where more achievement has nothing left to teach us. Men who put off failure indefinitely are more to be pitied than admired. Without access to their centres, they are condemned to circumference, to the half-life of the bottom-line.

The inspiration to do inner work begins where the success game ends: when our second marriage fails, or we go bankrupt, or there is some crisis about our health, or a loved one dies, or we get lost in an addiction, or some long-repressed emotion explodes to the surface. These cracks are powerful and expansive — powerful because they get our attention in a way that more success never could; expansive because they open us to questions of ultimate concern: Who am I? What am I here for?

The broken place is many things, but it is first of all an invitation: "Enter here."

If anger is your broken place, you have found your door. Gather up your resolve and go through it.

> *Don't turn your head. Keep looking*
> *at the bandaged place. That's where*
> *the light enters you.*
> **Rumi**

Blaming

Blaming is humanity's first and most enduring dysfunction. The Book of Genesis offers what is perhaps the first recorded instance of blaming: Adam blames Eve. Eve blames the snake. And the snake? To this day, most people get the creeps when they encounter one. Adam, ironically, remains a popular name for boys.

The mind is reflexively quick to transfer responsibility for a negative emotion, to assign blame, to make someone wrong so that we can, if only for a moment, experience the bliss of righteousness. This effort always involves a story, a one-act melodrama with victimized me in a starring role. *He did this to me. She lied to me. I can never forgive him/her for...* These stories do nothing to alleviate suffering; they only add to it.

There is great dignity in simply feeling a feeling without acting it out or projecting it onto someone else. To do this is to bear with serenity the pain of being displeasing to ourselves. To live is to suffer, after all. Mature men come to know and accept this; immature men waste a lot of time trying to make life easy.

The mind is a pain avoider. When you suffer with anger, the message from the mind is "You should not be suffering." It will immediately provide you with an escape from the unpleasantness of how you feel.

Or, if a scapegoat cannot be found, it may inspire you to ask "Why me?"

Well, why *not* me?

The stupidity of blaming is that it locates the source of my anger precisely where it cannot be solved — outside of and away from me. I need to start with myself. And end there, too. Inner peace is our greatest achievement. Anger cannot survive contact with peace. It hasn't got a chance.

A good man does not...

Explain. "Guilty, Your Honour, but with an explanation." Perhaps you have noticed that the guiltier one feels, the more urgently felt is the need to explain. You may also have noticed that the less effective the action, the more elaborate the rationale for it. Explanations are redundant. Our actions do not require commentary; they are perfectly eloquent in themselves. In the event you face criticism (fairly or not), first be aware of your need to be self-justified and righteous. If that is your motivation for talking, stop talking.

Discuss. The root of discuss is "to pick apart." In your heart, you already know what needs to be done — and, also, what is best left undone. You have always known what to do, and what not to do. Discussion is an unconscious and often ritualized form of self-doubt. It is also the first step toward argument. Say what needs to be said and leave it there.

Argue. This is ancient wisdom. Argument is catnip for men who are susceptible to anger. There are few more purposeless and destructive activities. Is it even a compliment anymore to be described as a man of strong opinions? How do you feel at the end of a "good" argument?

Good men do not argue.
Those who argue are not good.
Lao Tsu

All argumentation is a form of violence, a clash between the hosts of opposing mental positions. The purpose of the battle is to determine a winner and a loser. At the end of this exercise, one person will feel inflated, the other deflated. These are both negative outcomes. Nobody wins. Everybody loses.

If you are in any doubt about the futility of argument, watch two people as they argue. Notice what happens: the tension along the jaw, the set of the mouth, the stiffness in the body. If you really want to step out of the argument trap, notice yourself when you argue. That should do it.

Resistance

The way out of our cage begins with accepting absolutely everything about ourselves and our lives, by embracing with wakefulness and care our moment-to-moment experience. By accepting absolutely everything, what I mean is that we are aware of what is happening within our body and mind in any given moment, without trying to control or judge or pull away. I do not mean that we are putting up with harmful behavior — our own or someone else's. This is an inner process of accepting our actual present-moment experience. It means feeling sorrow or pain without resisting.
Tara Brach

It may sound like bad news to say resistance is futile, but, in fact, it is very good news. It means we don't have to get all heroic and go to war against what happens in our bodies. Such a war would be doomed to failure. Examine your own experience and see what you have gained, or more likely, lost, through acts of resistance. Recall that the first rule of martial arts is "Yield to overcome."

Acceptance (the positive term for non-resistance) may sound passive, even weak, but it is actually a dynamic state of being, the most powerful form of non-action you can practice. However, for acceptance to be acceptance it must be 100 percent, all or nothing. To say that you have partially accepted a condition means only that you continue to resist it.

Either you accept anger completely or you resist anger completely.

True acceptance means that you no longer require a condition to change. You are not wanting it to be different from the way it is. This is an expansive and open-hearted way to be. Whatever is, is allowed.

The miracle of acceptance is that *the condition we have stopped trying to change (because we have accepted it!) begins to change.* In the absence of our resistance, reconciliation and peace begin to flow. Anger cannot survive acceptance. It collapses like a leaky beach ball. What seemed a moment ago to be huge and menacing may now seem ridiculous. You may even find yourself laughing out loud.

When anger arises, let these be your watch words: resist nothing. Allow the anger to resonate within your body. Notice the tight circles of repetitive thinking that huff and puff in order to inflate the emotion. *Do nothing. Watch everything.* Feel the anger as it moves through you. When the anger is gone, be aware of how *that* feels.

The most enduring and mysterious symbol of non-resistance is water. Says Lao Tsu: "The highest good is like water." Water says "yes" to everything and "no" to nothing. It is the source and substance of life. Up to 70 percent of the human body is water. You could say we were designed for non-resistance!

None of this means that we cannot or should not take action if action is necessary. If action is required, then by all means take action. But let your action arise from acceptance. Action from acceptance has certain characteristics: It is free, spontaneous, powerful. It may be an action unlike any other you've ever done — full of grace, easy. Action that derives from resistance is the opposite — automatic, predictable, compulsive. Graceless and hard.

In all of our actions, without exception, the end is encoded in the means. Action from acceptance creates positive change; action from resistance perpetuates a cycle of suffering. We suffer when we resist what is, when we put ourselves in opposition to the facts of life. Be aware of how resistance feels. Stay with the feeling until there is nothing left to stay with. Then others can love you for the spaciousness that you are. And they will.

The impediment of hope

It is right in your face.
This moment,
The whole thing is handed to you.
Yuanwu

The biggest obstacle to acceptance is hope. Hope is resistance in its subtlest form, and any form of resistance, even one as pleasant-sounding as hope, takes you into suffering. How? Hope is future tense. It is the belief in the prospect of a better tomorrow. On the strength of our hope, we endure the Now. We do not embrace or transform it, we tolerate it. We wait, and we wait, and we hope.

All waiting achieves is more of the same, an extension of the status quo. It is an appeasement, a compromise, a way to avoid taking responsibility. Can peace, beauty and love be realized anywhere other than right here, right now? It is impossible. Life is now, and only now, and never not now. So give up hope. You have suffered enough.

When we give up hope we surrender to life. We stop holding on and start being held. There is no other way to discover the benevolence of life than by letting go and falling into it. Of course, the mind will rebel. It will create a raft of "What if...?" scenarios. Expect and allow that, but do not allow the machinations of mind to deter or dissuade you. Here is the promise of life: You will get what you need in the moment you need it. *But not before you need it.* That is not how life works.

If you give up hope, you will likely find your life is infinitely richer. Here's why: When you live in hope, it's usually because you're avoiding reality. If you hope your partner will stop drinking, aren't you really afraid he or she won't? Aren't you really afraid to take decisive action to change the situation? If you keep hoping the drinking will stop, you get to avoid the truly hard work of actually handling the situation effectively. Hope becomes a drug or soporific to get you through the pain a little longer. Like all drugs, it comes with side effects. One of the main side effects is that you become a little numb, a little less alive. Hoping a situation will change keeps you at a distance from your true feelings — sadness, anger, fear. Each of these feelings is best appreciated up close. Feel them deeply, and they will cease to bother you. Hope they'll go away, and they'll bother you all day.

Gay Hendricks

Anger is a signal

Signals have different messages but one basic demand: Pay attention. That is all anger requires — that we pay attention to it, that we acknowledge and respect its existence with our awareness. Men are not taught how to do this, or even that it is important to do. We are usually taught to act in exactly in the opposite way — not to acknowledge our feelings, but to stuff, bury or pack them away. The problem with this strategy is that there is no "away."

Feelings to which attention is not paid will inevitably work themselves out in the only other way possible, as a sickness, a chronic condition, or a difficult-to-treat set of symptoms. Some studies posit that chronic anger is more toxic to the body than smoking or over-eating.

Because the body is a limited actor, it reacts to anger in fairly typical ways — as tension, mostly, especially in the neck and shoulders, as nocturnal teeth grinding and erratic sleep cycles, as ulcers and acid reflux. Psychological symptoms are usually in alignment with the physical: impatience, cynicism, hyper-criticality, an inability to be still or to relax, workaholism, humourlessness, aggressive driving, risk-taking. It can also manifest in a generalized avoidance of life, in sleepiness and cynicism, laziness and indifference.

Frequently, the signs of anger are more apparent to others than to the one who is angry. Men who experience chronic anger and who have someone in their lives who loves them enough to tell them the truth — these are fortunate men.

The most important and transformative thing we can do is to pay attention to the inside. That's what is good about anger — it insists that we pay attention to what is happening within us. If our attention goes to the outside, we enter a fog of blame, projection, rationalization and denial.

Anger is a disturbance that is happening inside of me. It is not outside of me. The feeling I have is subjective, not objective. It's my problem. I own it. If I ignore or disown it, I will pay a price. In fact, I and those who love me have already borne the cost of my anger. So enough is enough. I will waste no more time condemning the outside. It is time to reorient myself. I see the world will not change until I do. Therefore, I bring my attention to the inside.

Now I get to explore what anger actually is. And I will discover that anger isn't what the psychiatrist described to me or what the workshop leader talked about. It's an occurrence that has certain qualities. It moves in certain parts of my body, and triggers certain kinds of feelings and memories, which all exist right now. Only now.
Steven Harrison

One thing at a time

When you do a thing, do it with the whole self. One thing at a time. Now I sit here and I eat. For me nothing exists in the world except this food, this table. I eat with the whole attention. So you must do — in everything.
George I. Gurdjieff

We have the ability to do only one thing well at a time. One of the most persistent yet least credible cultural myths is that of multi-tasking. Yes, it is possible to do two or three things at the same time. No, it is not possible to do any one of them well. And, in the attempt, we especially won't be well.

Anger asks for and requires nothing less than our full attention. The form and feeling of right now is the first priority. Always. There is no higher form of worship than devotion to the ordinariness of this little moment, christened "common magic" by the late Kingston poet Bronwen Wallace.

Anger needs conflict to survive

Conflict is anger's food. It is what anger needs to preserve itself. As conflict recedes, peace arises — a most threatening environment for anger. Although it is commonly held that opposites attract, this is not the case here. Peace and anger cannot coexist.

The lives of angry people are never free from conflict for long. That is because anger, like any other unconscious organism, is completely devoted to its own survival. There is nothing personal in this. Anger is only doing what it needs to do in order to survive. (Remember: *You are not anger.*)

To sustain and validate itself, anger needs regular contact with other forms of itself. Anger has an amazing radar; it becomes invigorated by, and unconsciously moves toward, the anger that exists in others. How else to explain how the two angriest guys on the road somehow find each other across four lanes in rush hour?

In some individuals, anger's appetite for conflict is so acute that they live on a sort of rolling boil, needing only for the temperature to rise a degree or two for rage to spill over. In others, conflict is mostly internalized. These men seem to exist on half-power, sleepy and stubborn and prone to addiction. In the first group, anger is directed out to become aggression; in the second group, anger goes in to become passive aggression. The first group goes to a counsellor's office; the second group rolls over and goes back to sleep.

The outer reflects the inner

Do you think you can take over the world and improve it?
I do not think it can be done.
Lao Tsu

The outer reflects the inner. Notice that the angry man lives in an angry world. The world he lives in is unbelievably generous — it supplies him day after day with a whole raft of reasons to be angry.

In contrast, the peaceful man lives in a peaceful world. Usually nobody takes much notice of the peaceful man. Where are the fireworks? The recriminations, resolutions and expressions of regret? Where is the drama: the shouting and yelling, the tears and the flowers?

A peaceful man embodies a state of being that anger cannot tolerate. Ironically, the angry man embodies the same state — he is just temporarily unaware of this unbelievable treasure. Real change happens from the inside out. This cannot be reversed — change on the outside does not produce change on the inside, at least not for long. If I win the lottery or move into my dream home, I will experience happiness, to be sure. But happiness is an emotion, and emotions cannot last because they are based on outer circumstances, and outer circumstances are as changeable as the weather. Events on the level of the outer cannot be relied upon. Nothing is permanent. Everything is passing away.

No matter what happens on the outside, my inner state will always assert itself. If I was miserable before I bought my Mercedes, I will soon be miserable while driving it.

No doubt we live in a dysfunctional, crazy world. No one who has ever watched television or read a newspaper can be surprised by this. But the world is not the problem. I am. The world will not change until I do.

> *...everything we see in the supposed outer world is really a reflection of — or a reaction to — our own state of being. If we look around and see anger, fear and suffering of all kinds, it is a result of the way we see, not what we see. Of course, horrible conditions exist, but being stuck on a superficial level, we can't see what underlies them: the vast presence in which all things have their existence. It is because of this incomplete way of seeing that each of us suffers in our own personal way... It is our own "knee-jerk" reactions — our tendencies to react out of fear or anger or selfishness to the events of our lives — that keep us spinning around.*
>
> **Krishna Das**

The anger addiction

Oh, yeah, it can feel *so good* to just let it out. To vent all that feeling in one big whoosh. Ahhhh, yes. So good.

So you feel better, do you? That's good, I guess. But what about the people around you who are now feeling a whole lot worse?

Projected anger is the crack cocaine of the emotional life.

One of the common misunderstandings about men's groups is that they are a place for troubled men to spill their guts. Although that might well happen in some clinical settings, my colleagues and I discourage it. It is just a lot easier and much more pleasant to work in a dump-free zone.

Venting anger does not resolve anger. It just leads to more venting. And more suffering. While it certainly provides short-term gratification for the individual, it inflicts long-term harm to his interpersonal environment. What feels like a therapeutic release to me can feel like assault to someone else.

There is often a post-vent recognition of damage done. This is where the high of release sinks to the low of regret. Frequently heard? "Let it go. Move on." (This is a typically masculine remedy — I have never heard these words, or a variation of them, from a woman.) The real meaning of "Move on" is "Forget about your pain." Not possible. All of our actions, from the smallest to the largest, have consequences. We cannot escape them.

The road to hell

Our intentions may be so good they gleam, but they are not by themselves a remedy for anything. It is a curious and contradictory defense, to justify a ruinous action by saying, "My intentions were good." The intention, after all, is revealed in the action.

Our culture is devoted to the notion that there is power in intention, e.g., "Whatever I believe, I can achieve." But there is a problem with this view. Neither power nor purpose is in the future. You want to be free from anger? Good. Now the goal ceases to matter. Only action matters. The end is right now, in the means.

To illustrate: My intention is to take a road trip from Montreal to Vancouver. When I step into the car, my intention ceases to matter. In fact, the more I focus on my intention (what I want in the future), the less attention I will have for the road (where I am right now).

The key is to *act without intention*. This is the primary teaching of one of the world's great wisdom books, the *Bhagavad Gita*. To focus on the action and not on the fruits of the action — on what the action is designed to achieve.

If we are honest with ourselves, we realize that we persistently view the present as a means towards an end... In this way the present is a commodity that we consume, manipulate and exploit; something we can use now to profit from it in the future. Even when we talk about inner work — seeing clearly, inquiring, investigating and seeing into things — our mind wants something from it. What would it mean to look at life without asking anything from it — even if for only a moment?

Christopher Titmuss

Talking

There is a wonderful (and comically repeated) line in the Woody Allen film *Bullets Over Broadway*. A playwright, drowning in delusion and self-importance, is desperately trying to express his existential angst to an equally self-centered actress. But before he has uttered more than a few words, she presses a hand over his mouth, looks deeply into his eyes and says, "Don't speak!"

Ah, yes. Don't speak. Good advice, especially when you are angry. But look what happens when anger dresses itself up to look like a virtue, as in the morality of truth-telling, as in "I've got to be honest," or "You may not want to hear this, but..." These words signify the imminent arrival of a verbal missile launched from some high peak of self-righteousness. They identify a speaker who employs honesty as a weapon. The intent of so-called straight talk is not to assist or illumine but to injure and diminish.

But I have to be honest! No, you don't. If all you have is honesty, you have nothing of value to contribute. It is far better not to speak.

Mere honesty inflates one person while deflating another. This is the opposite of communication, which means something held in common. One-way straight talk is the opposite of communication. It proceeds from a most dubious assumption: I am wise and you are stupid.

If you have doubt about whether to speak or not to speak, honour your reluctance.

You can never help one by telling about his faults, but you do him an injury, and injure yourself as well.
Vivekananda

For real communication (not pseudo-communication), two things must be present: honesty, yes, but humility most of all. Humility is the realization that what I dislike in another, what I desire to correct in someone else, is what I dislike about myself.

This can be a tough truth to swallow. But that's humility — a real leveler. We could call it tough love.

Why do you see the speck that is in your brother's eye, but do not notice the log that is in your own eye? Or how can you say to your brother, "Let me take the speck out of your eye," when there is the log in your own eye? You hypocrite, first take the log out of your own eye, and then you will see clearly to take the speck out of your brother's eye.
Jesus

Anger makes communication difficult but not impossible — indeed, when anger arises in the presence of a loved one, there is simultaneously a golden opportunity to communicate not your aggression (that's obvious) but your pain. To say, for example, *I feel angry about what just happened. It is painful for me to have this feeling, but I want to stay with it. Please allow me some space. Please bear with me. I will tell you when the feeling has passed.*

Typically, men have enormous difficulty expressing their feelings. Having a limited vocabulary to describe their emotions, they tend to be uncomfortable, embarrassed and clumsy-feeling when making the effort. In a therapeutic setting, as a sort of warm-up exercise, we may ask men to generate a list of 30 emotions. This light task can take a group of eight men 15 minutes to complete. Or to give up on. Sometimes, at the end of it, we ask the group how long it would take a group of women to do the same thing. That is always good for a laugh.

Three essential words

Yes. No. Maybe.

Let your "yes" be uncompromised and full of heart. Let your "no" be unwavering, of high quality, solid as stone.

If you do not know, do not commit. Life, to paraphrase Winston Churchill, is a riddle wrapped in mystery inside an enigma. It is okay not to know. There is wisdom — and roominess — in "maybe."

Listening

The highest, rarest and most healing form of communication doesn't involve talking at all. Listening is a form of reception. The best reception occurs when there is no competing electrical activity — no thinking — by the listener.

The listener who thinks while listening is pretending to listen. In actuality, he is analyzing content, assessing its value, formulating a response for when the speaker stops talking. If he were saying out loud what he is saying to himself, it would be called what it is: interrupting.

No one is really fooled by pseudo-listening — not for long, anyway. Something within us recognizes when we are being listened to. In the presence of true listenership, we physically relax. The words we release are unhurried and right. Anxiety falls away. We feel at home where we are.

The sole and essential pre-condition for true listening is inner space. By that I mean silence, stillness, the inner equivalent of an empty bowl. Stillness receives anything and everything. It does not judge, comment on, analyze or interpret. It simply allows.

When we truly listen, we give the precious gift of space. No relationship goes very deep without it. To be wordless and thoughtless together — what an extraordinary, accessible intimacy! In such a space, "I" and "thou" disappear — the two are one. As we approach that state, we become aware that nothing much needs to be said. When we enter that state, nothing *is* said. And nothing is left unsaid.

Thin ice

The most essential of the communication skills is the ability to speak up, to use the right words to effect positive change in a difficult situation. While easily learned, this vital skill is rarely taught. The hoped-for right words turn out to be the wrong words; a situation we want to improve is made worse. This must be a near-universal experience among men. I have many times in groups asked if anyone has *not* had this experience?

Richard Rohr once remarked that it's not a mistake to make a mistake — mistakes are how we learn and grow. As soon as a pattern of miscommunication has been acknowledged, it begins to change.

Gurdjieff taught that human beings have three centres: the brain, for mental activity; the heart, for relational/emotional activity; and the body, which converts into action the activity of the other two centres. The ideal form of verbal expression accounts for all of these centres. The following model of how to provide feedback accomplishes this in a very few words:

When you... (Describe the behavior you wish to change or stop — don't exaggerate or editorialize, just stick to the facts)

I feel... (mad, glad, sad — any feeling word, but just one) *because...* (Say why you feel that way.)

Example: When I ask you what's wrong and you say "Nothing," I feel angry because I know something *is* wrong.

Not surprisingly, "I feel..." is where most men stumble when they attempt to apply this formula. The reluctance of the male to name a feeling is worth inquiring into. It often exposes a dread of weakness or vulnerability.

There is no greater obstacle to communication than unacknowledged fear. In the naming of fear is the beginning of communication.

My story, my millstone

Men who elect to participate in our weekly group therapy sessions are given an orientation to the process before they begin. One of the things they are told is that this group is a story-free zone. This usually comes as a bit of a surprise because most men assume that's what a group is — a group of men sharing their stories. And, in lots of groups, that is exactly what happens.

Our goal as group facilitators is quite specific — we aim to keep men in the present moment as much as possible. The problem with stories is that they take us out of the present and into the past, which no one can do anything about. Stories about the past usually invoke multiple characters — ex- and current wives, bosses, parents, siblings and so on, none of whom are present.

Listening to a whole string of stories may make one feel surrounded by a host of ghosts. People are being conjured who cannot be seen, touched or talked to. We want men to bring their full attention to the flesh and blood of group — to the people they can see and interact with, to the life that is unfolding in front of them. The vitality of here-and-now is vastly more invigorating than the pseudo-life of there-and-then.

A therapeutic group is just a fancy term for right now. The task of the man who suffers with chronic anger is to tell the group when he is feeling impatient with another member, irritated by the instructor, frustrated by his lack of progress, or fed up with the whole business. The task of the repressed man is to say something out loud. Although everyone's task is different, each task will have an equivalent degree of difficulty. Not for nothing did Gurdjieff call this "doing the work."

"Here and now, boys," calls the piratical-looking bird in Aldous Huxley's *Island*. "Here and now." The same imperative could be structured in negative form as a Zen koan: If not here, where? If not now, when?

We step into our work when we step out of our story. The more attached we are to the story of me and my life, the less likely it is that we will undertake the work of transformation. The story weighs too much for us to progress very far. Who can travel any distance at all while carrying a dead elephant?

Most of us have a strong attachment to our story of what happened in the past, and often don't recognize how powerfully this story affects our lives. We are not only attached to memories of the good times, but also to memories of the bad times. There is a fear that if we let go of it, we will all be less interesting or that we won't know who we are anymore — that something important about us will die. In order to move into our full potential as human beings, there has to be a letting go of what we already know. Most people hang on to what they know for fear they won't survive. What keeps us stuck in the same old stories is that we never let them complete themselves. Waking up, the ability to live in the moment, is a dying of the old, the old way in which we perceive our lives. There has to be a stepping

out of our attachment to the past in order to discover who we are in
this moment.
Ariel and Shya Kane

In my experience, the most difficult story to let go of is the victim story — the story of how I have been wronged and unfairly treated by life. Men who are encased in a victim story cannot wait to tell you all of the details; they want you to know them as they know themselves, as a story. Do not inquire about who they are without their story because that threatens their identity, their frozen sense of who they are.

And yet, really, that *is* the question: Who are you without your story? Who...are...you?

The invitation...is really to stop telling your story. For one instant.
For less than an instant. Stop telling your story. Even if it is a good
story, just stop, and immediately the truth is told. You cannot tell
your story if you are telling the truth. And you cannot tell your truth
if you are telling your story. It is so obvious, isn't it.
Gangaji

A lousy question

If we could stop tampering with the universe we might find it a far better world than we think it to be. After all, we've only occupied it a few hundred million years, which is to say that we are just beginning to get acquainted with it. And if we continue another billion years there is nothing to assure us that we will eventually know it. In the beginning as in the end, it remains a mystery. And the mystery exists or thrives in every smallest part of the universe. It has nothing to do with size or distance, with grandeur or remoteness. Everything hinges upon how you look at things.
Henry Miller

"What's the problem?" That's a question I never ask of the men who present themselves for counselling. It's a lousy question. A problem suggests something that is perplexing or resolution-resistant, a psychological Rubik's Cube to be resolved only with the greatest degree of difficulty, and only then with the intervention of at least one expert.

The fact is that there really are no problems — there are only situations. A problem refers to something negative; a situation refers to something neutral. The approach to a situation can be light, even playful. By contrast, the approach to a problem is likely to be dense, complicated, risky. As a counsellor, my strong preference is to inhabit a problem-free zone. I cannot even imagine what it would be like to go to work and be required to deal with one problem after another!

During the course of everyday life, all sorts of situations arise, one after the other, many of which invite a response. So continuously do situations arise that we could fairly describe them as life's chief feature; however, to call them problems is to make life itself into a problem.

Calling life a problem activates a kick-back feature called karma by Eastern teachers. According to this ancient principle, whatever and whoever we treat as a problem will, in response, treat us as a problem. In other words, when we treat life as a problem, we are treated as a problem by life. Is this not an implacable truth?

Here are your options

As Tolle points out in *The Power of Now*, there are only two appropriate responses to a situation that is making you unhappy: You can speak up in order to change the situation. Or, if the situation cannot be changed, you can leave the situation. True, there may be certain situations which you can neither change nor leave — are you paralyzed, in prison, on death row? In those cases — that is, in situations of extreme limitation — you do the only thing possible: you accept the situation. One hundred percent.

Change it. Leave it. Accept it. What could be simpler? Or more sane?

What are you waiting for?

Now

Forget mistakes. Forget failures. Forget everything except what you're going to do now and do it. Today is your lucky day.
Will Durant

When you decide to change a situation, change it NOW. If you decide to leave a situation that cannot be changed, leave it NOW. Nothing happens outside of NOW. Whatever you do, you do NOW. NOW is the perfect time because NOW is the only time.

Change it or leave it, but do it NOW. There will be consequences — things will change. Accept the consequences; embrace the change. When we take action, we make a marvelous discovery — the world is truly a benevolent place. What your mind said was the worst thing you could possibly do, what it repeatedly warned you not to do, turns out to be the most life-giving thing you could have done.

Right now, and in every now-moment, you are either closing or opening. You are either stressfully waiting for something — more money, security, affection — or you are living from your deep heart, opening as the entire moment, and giving what you most deeply desire to give, without waiting.

If you are waiting for anything in order to live and love without holding back, then you suffer. Every moment is the most important moment of your life. No future time is better than now to let down your guard and love.

David Deida

A mild form of insanity

One of the least helpful things you can do about a situation is to complain about it. The literal meaning of complain is howl out loud. Complaining serves no purpose and is, frankly, beneath the dignity of mature men.

Complaining is a way to avoid changing the situation you are complaining about. It is a non-response masquerading as a response. Listening to a complainer is like entering into an unspoken conspiracy not to change anything by treating complaint itself as an action.

The sub-text of every complaint is the same: I do not want this to change. Sound crazy? It *is* crazy — insane, even. But it is a form of insanity so common that most people regard it as perfectly normal.

Anyone who does group work for long enough will encounter a character known as the help-rejecting complainer (HRC). This is a person with a tale of woe to share and, usually, a skillful way of telling it. The story is well-rehearsed, having been told and retold many times. Others offer advice, comfort, encouragement. The HRC expresses his appreciation and says he feels comfortable in the group. At the following session, members will want to know how the HRC is doing. Well, not so well, actually. Things are the same, maybe a little worse.

That is the HRC's story and, week after week, he sticks to it. Nothing ever changes; the rubber never hits the road. Eventually, the group will withdraw from the HRC, or the HRC will withdraw from the group. In fact, one of the ways to assess the functionality of a group is by the speed with which the group names the game of the HRC.

If you are in the presence of a complainer and are at the same time aware of your body, you may notice a loss of energy, a heaviness and fatigue. That is what happens when we enter the psychological equivalent of a black hole. There is less than no life in it.

Actions and reactions

I'm the decider.
George W. Bush

He [Saddam Hussein] tried to kill my daddy.
George W. Bush

The difference between an action and a reaction is the difference between yes and no. An action, emerging from a yes, is positive; a reaction, emerging from a no, is negative. Most self-described men of action are men of reaction. No-men. The judging "no" comes from the head. The allowing "yes" comes from the heart. Men of reaction crave certitude; they confuse vulnerability with weakness. Men of action are free to weep and not to know.

Reactions do not make challenging situations better — they make them worse. Reactions are a protest vote, an effort to deny what is. Imbedded within all reactions is the same thought: This should not be happening. Somebody must pay!

Action, by comparison, is relatively rare and utterly modest. It does not draw attention to itself, speechify, accept medals, collect honorary degrees. The secret and signature of action is that it deals with small things before they become big things. Around men of action, there is an aura of calm, not crisis. Around men of reaction, there is a sense of waiting for the next shoe to drop.

The man of action does only what is necessary, and he does it with surety and calm. Sometimes, the action is so subtle that onlookers may wonder if anything was done. Or they may think they did it themselves! If that is their conclusion, they will not be corrected by the man of action. He will probably agree with them.

Men of action say "yes" first. They see the facts and are undisturbed by them. If action is required, action is taken. If it is not required, they do not act. How beautifully simple this is. Men of action do not make reality into a problem. They immediately and calmly cooperate with the facts on the ground.

If reality is not a problem, there is less to do. Not nothing to do, just less to do. Men of action are unrushed and deliberate. They do not attempt to do two things at once. They embody the wisdom of Thoreau's caution: "Nothing can be more useful to a man than a determination not to be hurried." Men of action tend not to say they are busy. Being busy is beneath their dignity. They do not in conversation convey the sense of being late for a train, even if they *are* late for a train.

The man of action is restrained, understated, non-flamboyant. He knows the power of action withheld, of non-action. The ancient Chinese had an expression for this: *wu wei* or actionless activity. *Wu wei* is the bride, action the groom.

Who can wait quietly while the mud settles?
Who can remain still until the moment of action?
Lao Tsu

Let the past go

More suffering is caused by taking offence than by giving offence. Unavoidably, we give offence all the time — we cannot be in community and *not* give offence. Signals are missed, mistakes are made, egos collide. The offence we cause is most often unpremeditated and unintended. We are mostly unaware that offence has been taken. So frequently does this occur that if we knew in advance of the offence we would cause during the course of a day, it would be difficult to leave the house in the morning. It's been that way for a while:

> *Then Peter came up and said to him, "Lord, how often shall my brother sin against me, and I forgive him? As many as seven times?" Jesus said to him, "I do not say to you seven times, but seventy times seven."*
> **Jesus**

Forgiveness is little understood. Many people assume it must require great effort. And indeed it does if we believe in the existence of the past, if our mind is continually rehashing past injustices — "picking at old scabs," in the memorable phrasing of Robert Mumford. When that is the case, the best we can strive for is a sort of pseudo-forgiveness by which the one who "forgives" is rewarded with the mantle of the martyr.

If the past is dust, what is there to forgive?

True forgiveness takes no effort at all! If we are in right relation to our thoughts and do not take them altogether seriously, then forgiveness is as natural and as easy as breath itself.

Look lovingly upon the present,
For it holds the only things that are forever true.
All healing lies within it.
When you have learned to look on everyone with no reference at all
to the past,
Either his or yours as you perceive it,
You will be able to learn from what you see now.
To be born again is to let the past go,
And look without condemnation upon the present.
A Course in Miracles

Beliefs, opinions, principles

Don't seek enlightenment. Just cease to cherish your opinions.
Zen wisdom

As an exercise in group building, we sometimes ask men to take five or ten minutes to record on a piece of paper their three most unassailable beliefs, their rules of life, the principles in which they believe so devoutly that they could not under any circumstances be convinced to change or abandon them. Once these have been written down, the men read them out. Then we reflect on what has been done.

The first thing we observe is that no one in group has the same core values. This is the case even though most of the group are white, middle-aged or younger, middle-class, and live within easy driving distance of each other. And yet everyone's list is different. The differences may not be dramatic, but they are there.

We ask the group: What if the differences were extreme, even contradictory? What if the survey had revealed religious, sexual, political or cultural differences that put the holders of these values in positions of inevitable opposition? To what extent do individual beliefs predict the likelihood of conflict within the group?

We also inquire about the origin and durability of core values. Does the 32-year-old hold the same core values he did at 12? (No.) Are core values subject to change, displacement or irrelevancy. (Yes.) Could one live and be happy in the absence of core values, beliefs, principles? (Maybe.) The deeper we go, the fewer edges there are.

In the end, what does it matter, the difference between principles, beliefs, opinions and core values? All are thought-forms, mental formulae. If they are subject to change, modification or abandonment, none of them can be the truth. They are all staked out positions, bearing within them the seed of contrariness and disagreement.

An opinion is first cousin to a principle. You may have observed that opinions are not generally shared; they are discharged. Men in the grip of an opinion feel themselves to be the holders of an absolute truth. Some of the greatest stupidities ever spoken begin with the words, "This is the way it is." What follows is usually a partial truth masquerading as the whole truth.

An opinion gives verbal form to the need to be right. The need to be right is a barely submerged form of violence. I can be right only when someone else is wrong. Often, in the aftermath of some interpersonal meltdown, you will hear a protagonist say, "I was just expressing an opinion!" Well, exactly.

Conflict is inevitable when our thought structures assume a god-like significance. But our thoughts are not the truth. At best, they point to the truth; at worst, they become our Truth: We mistake the finger pointing to the moon for the moon itself. If we had some detachment, then our opinions would cease to matter so much. In its absence, we are liable to confuse what we think and believe with who we are. If our ideology is attacked, stepped on, ridiculed, it feels in the moment like we are being attacked, stepped on, ridiculed.

Rare indeed is the man who can say what he thinks without *becoming* his thoughts, who can lay his contribution on the table and leave it there. Whether his words are celebrated or laughed at matters little to him. He regards what he has just said with the same degree of detachment as he would if the words were someone else's. He has something to say but nothing to defend.

We are coming to the end of the age of ideology. We see this in the sudden, unpredicted collapse of political and financial structures. When we die, something similar happens — all of our opinions, belief systems and ideologies die with us.

In the absence of beliefs, would war ever happen? And what about love? Can we love without rules, beliefs, values, opinions?

Your gift to the world

Thirty spokes share the wheel's hub;
It is the centre hole that makes it useful.
Shape clay into a vessel;
It is the space within that makes it useful.
Cut doors and windows for a room;
It is the holes that make it useful.
Therefore benefit comes from what is there;
Usefulness from what is not there.
Lao Tsu

Your greatest gift to the world is not some-thing but no-thing. No-thing is emptiness, inner space. Space is life's most overlooked immensity. Without space, nothing that is could be. Men who cultivate spaciousness are unhurried and relaxed. They are not agenda-driven. They do what they do without a fuss. Spacious men have few (or no) beliefs to defend. They are emotionally porous; feelings pass through them like a breeze through sheers.

Space is easy to appreciate. Imagine: Sliding open the doors to your hall closet and finding it half-full, and with extra hangers! Imagine: A store room or basement that isn't crammed floor to ceiling with stuff.

Imagine: Walking from A to B in a straight line. Imagine: A horizontal surface with nothing on it. Increasing numbers of people dream of nothingness. Books on clutter-clearing now constitute a sub-specialty on the design shelves of major book stores.

On the inner level, space implies flow — a flowing through of thought and emotion. Thoughts enter and leave; they are not stored up or recycled. Emotions rise and fall modestly, easily, non-dramatically. When they are gone, they leave no trace.

When that happens, when the past leaves no trace, forgiveness has happened. True forgiveness happens by itself. If effort is required, it is not forgiveness.

Nothing fills up space faster than anger. Nothing creates space like its absence.

Spacious men are useful men. Not in the sense of watch-what-I-can-do, though they are invariably effective at whatever they undertake. They are men in whose company the best thing that could happen does happen.

Death

It is a good day to die.
Aboriginal peoples' saying

We are passing away. I am going to die, in a year or two or twenty. The number hardly makes much difference. It will be soon. You, too, are going to die. Also quite soon. If that fact makes you unhappy, life is your enemy. One you can't afford to have. Or get angry at.

Life and death are so intertwined they cannot be separated. We live in a culture largely blind to this fundamental unity. According to convention, death should not be spoken about unless absolutely necessary, and preferably in euphemistic terms, from the relatively plain "passed on" to the florid religiosity of "got translated into glory."

We befriend death when we acknowledge the impermanence of life in all of its forms, including our own. Endings are everywhere, imbedded in every experience and every relationship. If we protest these endings — of a relationship, of a job, of our physical abilities — we protest life itself.

Every ending is a "little death." We can practice dying, or letting go, every day. Men who struggle with anger are often poor with endings.

They hang on and hang on and call their hanging on a virtue. But there is nothing redemptive or responsible in this inactivity. Hanging on is just another way to avoid the work of self-transformation.

Endings are doorways to emptiness. Where there was something, now there is nothing. The impulse to flee is understandable, but nothing is life in its most sacred aspect, described in *The Tibetan Book of the Dead* as "the luminous splendour of the colourless light of Being." It is what the mystics call God.

The way in which we deal with life's endings predicts the manner of our own dying. Every single day offers multiple and subtle opportunities to practice the fine art of a good death.

Do you object? Good.

Can you die to your objection? Wonderful!

Breathe

Then the Lord formed man of dust from the ground, and breathed into his nostrils the breath of life; and man became a living being.
Genesis 2:7

The gift of breath is the gift of life. Nothing exceeds the value or power of the breath. It is easily our most potent and reliable ally, especially where anger is concerned. Consider its amazing abundance. If the average male takes 15 breaths per minute, he breathes 21,600 times during a 24-hour period. And yet he is usually unaware of even a single breath; his body, very kindly, does all of his breathing for him. What an extraordinary development, to have reached the point in our evolution as a species where we take completely for granted the greatest gift we will ever receive!

There are two kinds of breathing — conscious and unconscious. When our breathing is conscious, we are *aware* of breathing. When our breathing is unconscious, it happens automatically, without any awareness at all.

What does it mean to be aware of the breath? It means to notice the breath moving into and out of the body. To notice on the in-breath a coolness in the nostrils, the expansion of the abdomen, the slight pause before the out-breath. To notice on the out-breath the abdomen contracting, and the longer pause at the end of the emptying. The breath is neither controlled nor manipulated. It just happens as it happens. So we let it happen. We let it be.

The moment we become aware of our breath, respiration slows and deepens. At the same time, the body begins to relax, to release some of the tension it has been carrying. These are tremendously restorative changes — the breath moving from throat to diaphragm, the body releasing its tension — and they are immediately available to anyone *just by noticing the breath*.

Something else of great significance occurs during the act of taking a conscious breath: Thinking stops. If you have been telling yourself that you cannot stop thinking — well, yes, you can. Simply take one conscious breath, and in that moment you will have no thought, only the awareness of your breath. We cannot take a conscious breath and think at the same time. We do one or the other. We think or we breathe consciously.

It hardly needs saying that the mind will not celebrate the taking of a conscious breath. To the branch-jumping banana-eating monkey mind, it is a moment wasted. And yet consider what you have done — you have traded conditioned, compulsive thinking for the peace of pure space. You have stepped out of the mind and into awareness. This is a remarkable achievement.

I do not recommend that you make a rigorous discipline out of this, one more task to busy yourself with. Keep it simple. As often as it occurs to you, take one conscious breath. If you are an over-achiever and want to take two or three conscious breaths, that is fine, but it is not necessary. *The secret of conscious breathing is not how many conscious breaths you can take in sequence, but how often during the day you take them.* Frequency trumps duration. It is better to take five, seven or nine conscious breaths at different points during the day than to take the same number in a single sequence.

Each day will provide you with opportunities to take a conscious breath. The best time to do so is when you find yourself waiting — for an elevator, in a checkout line, in a traffic jam. Instead of thinking about where you need to be, be where you are. Breathe. In the taking of one conscious breath, you will experience a sense of aliveness, a spacious awareness, a peace. These sensations may be subtle at first, but the more often you breathe consciously, the deeper they will become.

Inner peace is your greatest achievement, and you achieve it by doing nothing at all. Lao Tsu describes your transformation as a "work without effort." Nice work if you can get it. And you can.

Do not wait until anger arises to take a conscious breath. If you wait until you have been seized with an emotion, its benefit will be slight. Begin *now*, when you are not angry, to be aware of your breathing. If this is all you do for your anger, for your peace, it will be many times more than enough.

But do not wait. Waiting only leads to more waiting. Start now.

We spend much of our time caught up in memories of the past or looking ahead to the future, full of worries and plans. The breath has none of that "other-timeness." When we truly observe the breath, we are automatically placed in the present. We are pulled out of the morass of mental images and into a bare experience of the here-and-now. In this sense, breath is a living slice of reality.
Henepola Gunaratana

Meditation

We have all tried all kinds of meditation techniques. We are still conflicted, neurotic, unfulfilled.

We sit down exhausted from our efforts, dispirited. We throw out the whole idea of meditating. We give up.

And there we are. We have finally come to where we are. Where we are is meditation, wherever we are.

Steven Harrison

Who could possibly count the number of books that have been written on the subject of how to meditate? This is a curious development because reading books about how to meditate bring us no closer to meditating than reading books about driving a car bring us to driving a car.

Meditation is simple. Just pay attention — that's all.

Meditation is paying attention to what is happening, wherever you are. You do not need to create a special environment for yourself, or invest in special chairs or cushions, or join a group. In fact, doing any of these things can actually create a barrier to meditation by making it seem special, esoteric, location-specific.

Meditation is paying attention to the everyday moments of everyday life. If you are doing something, pay attention to what you are doing. If you are thinking or feeling something, pay attention to that. Paying attention means being aware, awake, conscious.

Since you are interested in the challenge of anger, and since anger is a product of thought, you may want to start with your thinking.

The main point is to look straight at whatever thought arises, and relax. This is known as the meditation method in which there is no difference between someone who is learned and someone who is not.
Khenpo Tsultrim Gyamtso

The next time you become aware of a thought or a feeling, pay attention to it. Do this in a relaxed way. Notice what effect your sustained attention has on the thought or feeling.

One of the things you may notice is that *observed* thoughts and feelings don't hang around as long as *unobserved* thoughts and feelings. You may also feel less tense and more spacious, able to accommodate more of what comes without making a fuss about it.

What is the difference between meditation and living an ordinary human life? None at all, as far as I can see.

We often talk about "wanting to be spiritual," but being spiritual and taking care of everyday affairs are exactly the same thing. There is no difference. With clarity we become ordinary — simply taking care of whatever comes before us. In this process, we develop trust that whatever shows up in our lives, we will meet it.
Jacob Liberman

Last words

What looks like a demon is really a door. Anger cannot be denied, deflected or danced around. It has to be gone through. There is no other way.

It is a tight squeeze. The door symbolizes present-moment awareness. You are alert, ready, watchful. Jesus called this state of consciousness "the narrow gate." One that leads to the fullness of life, to the peace that cannot be understood.

When anger arises, know that the whole point and purpose of life is to give it your full attention. That is all. So focus on the feeling. Be aware of your thoughts. Very simple.

Your attention is everything. If you watch the feeling, you are out of the feeling. And if you are out of the feeling, what is the likelihood that you will indulge your anger? There is no likelihood at all.

The anger you consciously allow burns up tremendous amounts of inner resistance; the inner "no" that is responsible for the creation of anger in the first place is vastly weakened. Every time you suffer consciously, your capacity for anger is diminished. The good news is that the anger you go through is gone for good. And the process, once begun, is irreversible.

The space that is left when anger leaves is the clear space of pure consciousness. By simply becoming conscious of your anger, you have performed an alchemical act — the transformation of a toxic sludge into high-octane fuel. You have freed up energy for the enrichment of life. You have freed up yourself. Welcome home.

The lotus flower is one of the oldest symbols for the journey through anger and into radiant consciousness. This mysterious blossom takes root in the black muck at the bottom of a pond and then materializes on the surface as a cluster of unstained, luminous petals.

No muck, no flower. No anger, no peace.

Blessings on the way.

Sources

Almaas, A.H. *The Pearl Beyond* Price. Reprinted by arrangement. Shambhala Publications Inc., 1998. www.shambhala.com

Balsekar, Ramesh S. *A Net of Jewels*. Reprinted with permission. Advaita Press, 1996. www.advaita.org; www.ramesh-balsekar.com

The Bible, Revised Standard Version. Matthew 7:3, 18:1-3, 18:21-22.

Brach, Tara. *Radical Acceptance*. Bantam Books, 2003. www.imcw.org

Brother Lawrence. *Ordinary Graces*. Pickwick Publications, 1989.

Cohen, Leonard. "Anthem" from *Stranger Music: Selected Poems and Songs*. McClelland & Stewart, 1994. www.leonardcohen.com

A Course in Miracles—Gifts from a Course in Miracles. Edited by Frances Vaughn and Roger Walsh. Tarcher-Putnam, 1995.

Gangaji. www.gangaji.org

Gunaratana, Henepola. *Mindfulness in Plain English*. Wisdom Publications, 1993. www.bhavanasociety.org

Gurdjieff: Essays and Reflections on the Man and His Teaching. Edited by Jacob Needleman and George Baker. The Continuum Publishing Company, 1997.

Gyamtso, Tsultrim Khenpo. *The Three Nails, Part II*. Translated by Ari Goldfield. Reprinted by permission. *Bodhi Magazine*, Vol. 4, Issue #1, Part 2, 2001. http://ktgrinpoche.org

Harrison, Steven. *Getting to Where You Are*. Tarcher-Putnam, 1999. www.doingnothing.com

_____. *The Question to Life's Answers*. Sentient Publications, 2002.

_____. *Being One*. Sentient Publications, 2002.

Hendricks, Gay. *A Year of Living Consciously*. HarperSanFrancisco, 1998. www.hendricks.com

Huxley, Aldous. *Island*. Harper and Row, 1962. http://somaweb.org

Katie, Byron. www.thework.com

Krishnamurti, J. *On God*. HarperCollins Publishers, 1992. www.kfa.org; www.kfoundation.org

Lao Tsu. *Tao Te Ching*. Translated by Gia-Fu Feung and Jane English. Vintage Books, 1989.

Liberman, Joseph. *Wisdom from an Empty Mind*. Empty Mind Publications, 2001.

Locker, Thomas. *Walking with Henry*. Reprinted with permission. Fulcrum Publishing, 2002.

Lozoff, Bo. *It's a Meaningful Life*. Viking, 2000. www.humankindness.org

Matthiessen, Peter. *The Snow Leopard*. Viking, 1978.

Miller, Henry. *Standing Still Like the Hummingbird*. New Dimension Books, 1962. www.henrymiller.org

_____. *The Wisdom of the Heart*. New Directions, 1941.

_____. *Plexus*. Grove Press, 1987.

Moore, James. *Gurdjieff: The Anatomy of a Myth*. Element, 1991.

Morrison, Scott. *The Gentle, Passionate Art of Not-Knowing*. Renaissance Memes, LLC, 2000.

Packer, Toni. *The Light of Discovery*. Charles E. Tuttle Co., 1991.

Ram Dass. *Paths to God: Living the Bhagavad Gita*. Random House, 2004.

Rilke, Rainer Maria. *Letter to a Young Poet*. Translated by Stephen Mitchell. Random House, 1986.

Rohr, Richard and Joseph Martos. *The Wild Man's Journey*. St. Anthony Messenger Press, 1996.

Rumi, Jelaluddin. *The Essential Rumi*. Translated by Coleman Barks with John Moyne. HarperCollins/Castle Books, 1995.

Titmuss, Christopher. *The Awakened Life*. Shambhala Publications Inc., 2000.

Tolle, Eckhart. *The Power of Now*. Reprinted with permission. New World Library, 1999. www.newworldlibrary.com; www.eckharttolle.com

Trungpa, Chögyam. *Cutting Through Spiritual Materialism*. Reprinted by arrangement. Shambhala Publications Inc., 1973. www.shambhala.com

Yuanwu. *Zen Wisdom*. Translated by Thomas Freke. Godsfeld Press, 1997.

Watts, Alan. "This Is It" from *The Way of Liberation*. Vintage Books, 1973. www.alanwatts.com

Welch, Lew. *Ring of Bone: Collected Poems 1950-1971*. Grey Fox Press, 1973.

Keith Ashford, M.Div.

Keith Ashford is a teacher, speaker
and counsellor. A former journalist
and minister, he has provided group
and individual counselling services
to men since 1992. He has taught
extensively on personality patterns and
is currently at work on an Enneagram-
related book called *Masked Men: Nine
Personality Types*. He and wife Marilyn
live in Kingston, Ontario.